Back to the Sources

by

MARIANNA NUGENT PRICHARD

and

NORMAN YOUNG PRICHARD

UNITED CHURCH PRESS

Boston, Philadelphia

Pronunciation Guide

ä	calm	ī	kite
ă	sat	ō	over
à	arise	ŏ	on
ā	ate	ô	orb
ĕ	met	ŭ	up
ē	mete	û	urge
ĭ	sit	ū	rule

Scripture quotations, unless otherwise indicated, are from the *Revised Standard Version of the Bible,* copyrighted 1946 and 1952 by the Division of Christian Education, National Council of Churches, and used by permission.

This book is part of the United Church Curriculum, prepared and published by the Division of Christian Education and the Division of Publication of the United Church Board for Homeland Ministries.

Library of Congress Catalog Card Number 64-19464

Contents

The church began with Christ and his disciples, shown here in a detail from a
fourth-century sarcophagus in Aix-en-Provence, France

Your church is important to you. As a baby you were probably baptized in church, and more than likely you have been, or soon will be, confirmed as a full church member. No doubt you will someday be married in church. At every important milestone in your life the church is there, encouraging you, offering you wisdom and strength, speaking to you God's word of challenge, judgment, forgiveness, and blessing.

Why? How did the church happen to be there waiting for you when you were born? Why is the church at work now?

It's a long story—more than two thousand years long—and it is still unfolding. Every chapter was headline news when it happened, and it still makes exciting reading. In this book you will find the comments of those who actually lived the story. You will read Benedict's hopes for the monastery he was organizing. You will hear some of Luther's own words that sparked the Protestant Reformation. You will learn what the Massachusetts Puritans asked of prospective church members, and read a letter from a twentieth-century Christian martyr in China.

An old story—but new as tomorrow. For it is your story. You may be in the next chapter of the story of the Christian church—you and your contemporaries and God. When you have read these earlier chapters of your story, you will know yourself better. You will have a clearer vision of what the next chapter can be, the chapter you can help to write.

What is the church? Is it just a large building, handsome or not so handsome, which we can line up with many other buildings that influence our lives—our high school, our county courthouse, our hospital, the Second National Bank? Or is our church more, infinitely more—the holy fellowship that undergirds us with love and points us to Christ, the pole star of the world around whom our lives must move and in whose service we can find meaning, joy, and freedom for living? What *is* the church? What is its job in the world?

WHAT ABOUT THE CHURCH?

Do teenagers need the church? The following report comes from an urban church in California. What is the church saying to the young people there?

One day Stanley, one of the many boys, out of school and unemployed, . . . who are helping us from day to day here in the church, came to me and said, "There's a whole bunch of guys meeting in the park." I went to the park and met a group of about forty boys who were obviously having some sort of organized meeting. I went up to the leader, explained our desire to open the church weekdays after school for a teen-canteen. I suggested that they could come immediately over to the church. I left them in the park and returned to the church (just seventy-five feet away) and waited an agonizing forty-five minutes. Then they arrived, all of them. They came in the door, fearful, suspicious, hesitant. Soon, however,

the blaring jukebox had them comforted, the ping-pong table was clicking away, . . . and after bidding every one of them welcome I retreated to an adjacent room. . . .

Soon, the president came in and asked, "Are you really a minister?" I assured him that I was. He returned a few minutes later and asked, "What kind of a church is this?" A few minutes, and some conversation later, he returned a third time and asked, "How much is it going to cost?" I told him that we were opening the church building to him because he belonged here; that there would be no "charges." He discussed this new bit of information with his friends again. Meanwhile, they began running all over the building exploring a church, a new experience for most of them. When he returned to me a fourth and last time he said, "I noticed you have been painting. Do you want some help?" I could hardly answer, the lump in my throat was too big, as I thanked God for what was happening. And so they began to come, sometimes in groups of four or five. Sometimes, like yesterday, we had one hundred and fifty. Our average attendance at the canteen for the last few weeks has been about forty.

***

We have promised the boys and girls of our street that we would develop a school for dropouts, completely separate from the regular high school program of our city. They have almost unanimously indicated their desire to return to school on such a basis. When I was in the street trying to settle a fight, a carload of older boys came by in a white T-Bird and asked if our "school" was going to be ready soon. Sadly, I had to tell them that we had no money as yet.

Can the church meet the needs of today's teens? How can you help? What part do you play in your church's ministry to the world?

HOW BIG IS JOE'S CHURCH?

Five years ago if I had asked Joe, "How big is your church?" he might have answered me, "About four times as big as my house." *Church* would have meant to him the steepled brick building at the corner of Main and Third where he met with his junior class in church school once a week.

If I had asked Joe that same question last year, he might have answered, "Oh, about five hundred members, I guess." He had made progress. *Church* now meant, not brick and mortar, but a group of people, his own congregation, worshiping God together in Joe's hometown. Joe knew, of course, that there were other churches besides this one congregation in his town—the Episcopal Church, the Nazarene, the Roman Catholic, the Serbian Orthodox. But he wouldn't have thought of those groups as connected in any way with his church. Their buildings looked so different, their ways of worship were so unlike his own. Five miles out in the country is another church with the same denominational name as Joe's, but last year Joe wouldn't have thought of himself as being in the same Christian fellowship with the people of that group either. He didn't know them. His idea of *church* wasn't big enough to take them in.

That was last year. In the meantime Joe spent a week at camp with nearly a hundred other young people of his denomination, many from communities hundreds of miles away from Joe's. How big did Joe's church grow during that week as he learned to know

4

these new friends? He discovered how thousands in his denominational family across the country were working together to share the good news of Jesus Christ with people in many different parts of the world. He learned of efforts to make local communities more Christian, and to bring justice to those who are oppressed. The walls of Joe's church pushed out far beyond his old understanding.

One of Joe's new friends, slightly older than the others, was a ministerial student named Yuji Sato. He had attended a Japanese college founded with the help of missionaries of Joe's denomination. But Yuji didn't call himself a member of that denomination. No, he said he belonged to the United Church of Christ in Japan, a fellowship of people of many different denominational backgrounds. Yuji said he wished his church were even broader—that it would include all the Christian people of Japan. Yuji was a great believer in the *ecumenical* (ĕk-ū-mĕn′ĭ-kŏl) church. He described it as the one great fellowship of Christians everywhere in the world who acknowledge Christ as their Lord and try to do his will. Yuji said that the ecumenical church reaches across the barriers that separate local congregations, denominations, and countries. It is bigger than all the national councils of churches in all the world's nations, though these councils help to make the ecumenical dream come true. It is bigger than the World Council of Churches. It is as big as the mind and spirit of Christ, binding all of Christ's people together in love.

5

When Joe got back from camp, he found that he felt a little closer to the Episcopalians, the Nazarenes, the Roman Catholics, and the Serbian Orthodox people in town. Were they also part of the ecumenical church of which Yuji spoke? Was Joe, too?

If I would say today, "Joe, how big is your church?" I wonder what he would answer.

WHAT IS THE CHURCH SAYING TO OUR WORLD?

What is the church saying to our world? What does it say to a homesick fifteen-year-old girl who has come as a refugee out of China into the crowded, reeking alleys of Hong Kong? What does

it say to a Japanese medical student who has had to drop out of school to support his crippled father? To an American storeowner who would like to keep his business strictly honest, but is tempted to overcharge a little and to falsify a few labels to get the money to put his two daughters through college? What is the church saying to me?

The apostle Paul once told a panic-stricken jailor who had just tried to kill himself, "Believe in the Lord Jesus, and you will be saved." (Acts 16:31) Does the church still say that to people now?

The Hong Kong teenager hears a Christian pastor speak of this Jesus who said, "I was hungry and you gave me food." (Matthew 25:35) She volunteers to help in a Church World Service feeding center handing out cups of milk to a line of scrawny little children every afternoon. Jesus Christ seems very real to her as she works. He has shown her a way out of futility.

The Japanese medical student wanders into a Christian student center in Tokyo and hears a classmate reading, "In the world you have tribulation; but be of good cheer, I have overcome the world." (John 16:33) Suddenly he begins to feel that God will somehow open a pathway through his difficulties. He goes home heartened.

The American storeowner is reading Luke, preparing to teach a church school class. He stops short at Jesus' words about the man who "lays up treasure for himself, and is not rich toward God." He reads on, "For all the nations of the world seek these things; and your Father knows that you need them. Instead, seek his kingdom, and these things shall be yours as well." (Luke 12:21, 30–31) He frowns, pondering. Jesus has underlined a truth for him. His daughters need college, of course, but even more they need a father with self-respect and integrity.

Can you hear the church saying to each of these people, "Jesus Christ is the way, the truth, and the life. Believe in the Lord Jesus Christ, live by the love he revealed, and you will be saved." Is this the church's message to the world, spoken in different ways to different people with their various needs and problems? How is the church bringing its message to you? How do you, speaking for your church, speak its message in your world?

What do we uncover when we probe into the dramatic beginnings of the Christian church? A group of frightened, leaderless disciples cringing after Good Friday's tragedy? A few heroic men testifying to their risen Christ, sworn to his new covenant even if it should cost them their lives? A fellowship trying out the forms of worship, service, and church government that seem nearest to the mind of Christ?

THE COVENANT TAKES ON NEW MEANING

I, ———, take thee, ———, to my wedded wife, to have and to hold from this day forward, for better for worse, for richer for poorer, in sickness and in health, to love and to cherish, till death do us part, according to God's holy ordinance; and thereto I plight thee my troth.

So reads the covenant of marriage that joins two persons in holy wedlock.

Our idea of binding two parties as one in covenant relationship has its roots in the Hebrew experience of God even as far back as the time of Abraham in the Tigris-Euphrates valley. The Lord God covenanted with Abraham that they would be "wed" to each other. God promised to make of Abraham and his descendants a great people. Long years later some of Abraham's descendants found themselves slaves in Egypt. God sent a new leader, Moses, to lead these captive Israelites out of bondage. He brought them into the wilderness of Sinai where God renewed his covenant with them, binding them anew to himself as his covenant people. The Ten Commandments, the social precepts of God's covenant community, helped keep the Hebrews aware of this covenantal relationship.

Twelve hundred years later Jesus took a cup and said, "This is my blood of the new covenant." (Mark 14:24) He redefined the old Hebrew concept of the covenant. Jesus saw the people of the new Israel bound together not by blood ties or language or territory, but by faith in him. The new Israel included *all* those who were to believe in him as God's Messiah, all who would be gathered together in the faith. The ceremonial rite of circumcision had been the symbol of the old covenant. Now the communion cup became the symbol of the new covenant. That communion cup would serve in place of a wedding ring for the Christian church which thought of itself as the bride of Christ, bound to him in covenant.

At the beginning of the Judeo-Christian drama, God and Israel were bound together by the solemn promises of the old covenant. Now, through Jesus, the Christ, God was with the new Israel. A new covenant had been established.

You, as a twentieth-century Christian, are involved in that new covenant. It binds you to Christ through faith in his power to re-

The covenant was sealed at Jesus' last supper, shown here in a thirteenth-century mosaic from the Basilica of San Marco, Venice

deem your life from prideful selfishness. It commits you to work in thankful love for the coming of Christ's kingdom of good will and peace on earth. It unites you in faith with all Christians from the first small group in Jerusalem to the worldwide church of the space age. What does this new covenant really mean to you?

WHO ARE THESE CHRISTIANS?

Imagine yourself a conscientious Roman magistrate in A.D. 150. It has come to your attention that Christians in your jurisdiction are refusing to worship the emperor, and you want to learn what sort of people these Christians really are. Trying to forget the ugly rumors you've heard about Christianity, you ask four witnesses the four questions that follow. The early Christian writers quoted below tell us how your witnesses would probably have answered.

Who are the leaders?

Having, therefore, received their orders, and being fully assured by the resurrection of our Lord Jesus Christ, and established in the word of God, with full assurance of the Holy Ghost, they [the apostles] went forth proclaiming that the kingdom of God was at hand. And thus preaching through countries and cities, they appointed their first-fruits, having proved them by the Spirit, to be bishops and deacons of those who should afterward believe.[1]

—Clement of Rome, c. A.D. 96

How are new Christians initiated?

As many as are persuaded and believe that the things are true which are taught and said by us, and promise that they are able to live accordingly, they are taught to pray and with fasting to ask God forgiveness of their former sins, while we pray and fast with them. Thereupon they are brought by us to where there is water, and are born again in the same manner of a new birth as we, also, ourselves were born again. For in the name of God the Father and Lord of all, and of our Saviour Jesus Christ, and of the Holy Spirit, they then receive the washing in the water.[1]

—Justin Martyr, c. A.D. 150

10

How do Christians worship?

And on the day called the Day of the Sun there is a gathering in one place of us all who live in cities or in the country, and the memoirs of the Apostles or the writings of the prophets are read as long as time allows. Then, when the reader has ceased, the president gives by word of mouth his admonition and exhortation to imitate these excellent things. Afterward we all rise at once and offer prayers; and as I said, when we have ceased to pray, bread is brought and wine and water, and the president likewise offers up prayers and thanksgivings as he has the ability, and the people assent, saying "Amen." The distribution . . . and partaking . . . then take place; and to those not present a portion is sent by the hands of the deacons. Those who are well-to-do and willing give, every one giving what he will, according to his own judgment, and the collection is deposited with the president, and he assists orphans and widows, and those who through sickness or any other cause are in want.[1]

—Justin Martyr, c. A.D. 150

How do Christians behave?

They do not commit adultery or fornication, nor bear false witness, . . . nor covet what is not theirs. They honor father and mother and show kindness to their neighbors. . . . They do not worship idols made in human form. . . . And their oppressors they appease and they make friends of them; they do good to their enemies. . . . If they see a stranger, they take him to their dwellings and rejoice over him as over a real brother. . . . And if they hear that one of them is imprisoned or oppressed on account of the name of their Messiah, all of them care for his necessity, and if it is possible to redeem him, they set him free. And if any one among them is poor and needy, and they have no spare food, they fast two or three days in order to supply him with the needed food. . . . Every morning and every hour they acknowledge and praise God for His lovingkindness toward them.[1]

—From the "Apology" of Aristides, c. A.D. 125

11

THE FIRST THREE HUNDRED YEARS ARE THE HARDEST

It is always easy to distrust people with peculiar ways of acting and thinking. The ways of the Christians were so radically different from those of their Roman neighbors that the magistrates were horrified. Christians would not serve in the army. They would not abandon unwanted babies, attend brutal gladiatorial games, take their disagreements to a law court, or sprinkle incense on the emperor's altar. They trusted in the power of love. As thousands were won to the new religion, it was obvious that the power of love was undermining the power of Roman force. So Rome struck back with more force for nearly three hundred years—and gave the church thousands of martyrs.

The names of the martyrs became watchwords among the early Christians, nerving them for struggles within themselves and fearful testings in the outside world. One of the most revered of these martyrs was Polycarp (pŏl' ĭ-kärp), the gentle old bishop of Smyrna (smŭr'nà). In his younger days, Polycarp had talked with Jesus' disciples, and he passed on to the church his cherished memories of these conversations. A letter sent from the church at Smyrna tells how Polycarp met death in A.D. 155.

Mounted police with their usual arms . . . found him in a cottage, lying in an upper room. He could have gone away to another farm, but he would not, saying, 'The will of God be done'. So, hearing their arrival, he came down and talked with them, while all that were present marveled at his age and constancy, and that there was so much ado about the arrest of such an old man. Then he ordered that something should be served for them to eat and drink. . . . And he besought them that they should grant him an hour that he might pray freely. They gave him leave, and he stood and prayed . . . and the men repented that they had come after so venerable an old man.

When he had brought to an end his prayer, in which he made mention of all, small and great, high and low, with whom he had had dealings, and of the whole Catholic Church throughout the world, the time had come for him to depart. And they set him on an

ass and led him into the city. . . . Now, as he was entering the sta-
dium, there came to Polycarp a voice from heaven, 'Be strong, Poly-
carp, and play the man' . . . the Proconsul tried to persuade him, . . .
'Say, "Away with the atheists!" ' Then Polycarp looked with a se-
vere countenance on the mob of lawless heathen in the stadium, and
he waved his hand at them, and looking up to heaven he groaned
and said, 'Away with the atheists.' But the Proconsul urged him and
said, 'Swear, and I will release thee; curse the Christ.' And Polycarp
said, 'Eighty and six years have I served him, and he hath done me
no wrong; how then can I blaspheme my king who saved me?' . . .

Then said the Proconsul, 'I have wild beasts; if thou repent not,
I will throw thee to them.' But he said, 'Send for them.' . . . Then
said the Proconsul again, 'If thou dost despise the wild beasts I will
make thee to be consumed by fire, if thou repent not.' And Polycarp
answered, 'Thou threatenest the fire that burns for an hour and in a
little while is quenched; for thou knowest not of the fire of the judg-
ment to come, . . . But why delayest thou? Bring what thou wilt.' . . .
He was filled with courage and joy; and his countenance was full of
grace, . . .

When he had ended his prayer the firemen lighted the fire.[2]

THE MARTYRDOM OF
SAINT POLYCARP
a fifteenth-century woodcut

13

Jesus had changed all of life for his followers. His life, death, and resurrection had flooded their lives with meaning. Who was this strangely powerful personality? A mere human being? A ghost? What did God mean by sending him to earth? This man who had proved mightier than almighty death, did he somehow share in the nature of the eternal God himself (staggering thought!)? These are the questions men had to wrestle with in the young church. Are their answers meaningful to us today?

SOME OFF-BEAT IDEAS AND A PASSWORD

Sometimes we twentieth-century Christians worry over differences of opinion about the basic meaning of our faith. Roman Catholics think one way and Protestants another. Fundamentalists disagree with liberals. Perhaps you and your friends have "argued religion." We do not think alike and we despair of getting together. But if we study Christian thinking in the days of the early church, we can see the progress we have made toward basic agreement since then.

Leaders of the early church had more than Roman lions to worry about. Far more dangerous to the Christian faith were the ideas circulating among some Christians—ideas reflecting Greek philosophy and Persian and Egyptian religions. Lumped together, these ideas are called Gnosticism (nŏs' tĭ-sĭzm).

The Gnostics believed the physical world was evil, something that a good God could not have created. The world must have been the work of an impure spirit, not the Father of our Lord Jesus Christ. Because they believed that physical things were evil, the Gnostic Christians thought Jesus could not actually have had a physical

Drawing of a Gnostic seal representing the two powers battling to control the world

body that died on the cross; he had only appeared to have one. The Gnostics believed that the good God was he of whom the New Testament spoke; the creator God of the Old Testament was an inferior, evil spirit called the Demiurge. According to Gnostic thought, these two powers were always battling for control of the universe and of men.

Early church leaders in Rome saw that they must do something drastic about this Gnostic propaganda. First, they drew up a statement of basic Christian beliefs that were not to be tampered with; and second, they excommunicated leaders who taught ideas contrary to those beliefs.

Their statement of beliefs was termed the Roman symbol. A symbol was a military password. Bishops asked new "Christian soldiers" to accept the "password" before they were baptized into the church. By the sixth century the Roman symbol had been altered and expanded into what we know as the Apostles' Creed.

THE APOSTLES' CREED

I believe in God the Father Almighty, maker of heaven and earth, and in Jesus Christ his only Son our Lord, who was conceived by the Holy Ghost, born of the Virgin Mary, suffered under Pontius Pilate, was crucified, dead, and buried. He descended into hell; the third day he rose again from the dead; he ascended into heaven, and sitteth on the right hand of God the Father Almighty. From thence he shall come to judge the quick and the dead.

I believe in the Holy Ghost, the holy catholic church, the communion of saints, the forgiveness of sins, the resurrection of the body, and the life everlasting. Amen.

15

Arius argues his point   Eric Von Schmidt

CONSTANTINE SETTLES (?) AN ARGUMENT

The Roman symbol had stated that Jesus was truly man. But was he also truly God? A bitter debate developed over this question, with Athanasius (ăth-à-nā′shĭ-ŭs) heading the affirmative team and Arius (ăr′ĭ-ŭs) heading the negative. The controversy between Arius and Athanasius was in part an argument between two towns that debated for hundreds of years. Arius came from Antioch, and like many Antiochian Christians, he believed that Jesus was human as we are. Jesus was like God in his goodness, he was God's word, but he was not God himself. Here is what Arius wrote to a friend concerning the controversy:

Athanasius defends orthodoxy   Eric Von Schmidt

*Alexander has driven us out of the city [of Alexandria in Egypt]
as atheists, because we do not concur in what he publicly preaches;
namely, "God is always, the Son is always; . . . the Son is of God
himself." . . .*

*To these impieties we cannot listen even though heretics threaten
us with a thousand deaths. But we say and believe and have taught
and do teach, that the Son is not unbegotten, . . . that before He was
begotten . . . He was not. . . . We are persecuted because we say that
the Son has a beginning, but that God is without beginning. . . . He
is neither part of God, nor of any substance. . . . For this we are persecuted; the rest you know. I bid thee farewell in the Lord.*[1]

Arius went to Alexandria sometime before A.D. 311 to expound his theory, and here he ran into trouble. People in Alexandria insisted that Jesus certainly *was* God, quite as much so as God the Father. He was truly God *and* truly man. A young Alexandrian priest named Athanasius defended this view so ably that it became known as the Athanasian belief.

Very shortly Christians in many cities of the Roman empire became passionately involved in this dispute. It raged hotter and wider, until Emperor Constantine grew much alarmed. He had backed Christianity in the hope that this popular new religion could hold his shaky empire together, but now Christians were at one anothers' throats, splitting the empire in two. Constantine decided to settle the matter.

He called together a council of bishops at Nicaea (nī-sē'á) in A.D. 325. More than three hundred bishops came from places as far apart as Mesopotamia and Spain. They started the meeting in a church, but two weeks later when Emperor Constantine arrived in town, they moved into a palace to welcome him properly as he entered the assembly in his imperial robes.

Arius' party presented a creed, but the majority rejected it completely; later on they voted to excommunicate Arius and burn his writings. Athanasius' conception of God as a trinity of Father, Son, and Holy Spirit proved to be much more popular. The Nicene delegates adopted a creed (the Nicene symbol) featuring this trinitarian description of God. They also insisted that Jesus was *of one and the same substance with* God, not merely *like* God. The statement we call the Nicene Creed actually comes from a somewhat later time, but it reflects the ideas of the Nicene symbol worked out by Constantine's ecumenical council.

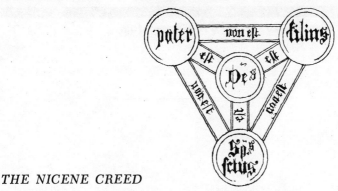

THE NICENE CREED

I believe in one God the Father Almighty, Maker of heaven and earth, and of all things visible and invisible:

And in one Lord Jesus Christ, the only-begotten Son of God, begotten of his Father before all worlds, God of God, Light of Light, very God of very God; begotten, not made, being of one substance with the Father, by whom all things were made; who for us men and for our salvation came down from heaven, and was incarnate by the Holy Ghost of the Virgin Mary, and was made man; and was crucified also for us under Pontius Pilate. He suffered and was buried; and the third day he rose again according to the Scriptures; and ascended into heaven, and sitteth on the right hand of the Father. And he shall come again, with glory, to judge both the quick and the dead; whose kingdom shall have no end.

And I believe in the Holy Ghost, the Lord and Giver of life, who proceedeth from the Father and the Son; who with the Father and Son together is worshiped and glorified; who spake by the prophets. And I believe one holy catholic and apostolic church. I acknowledge one baptism for the remission of sins; and I look for the resurrection of the dead, and the life of the world to come. Amen.

The Christian life was hard and demanding, as hard for a young man in the fifth century as it is for us now. Augustine found it so impossible to resist the temptation to lust that he concluded that only God's grace could conquer this evil in his life. And God's grace did. Augustine's joy in the strength that comes to us through Christ's love was the song that he sang to the world in his *Confessions*. Have we discovered this song for ourselves? Are we citizens of the city of God, the joyous fellowship of the redeemed, about whom Augustine wrote? Do we agree with Chrysostom as to how citizens of that city should treat their fellowmen?

NORTH AFRICA'S MOST FAMOUS JUVENILE DELINQUENT

Monica, deeply Christian mother though she was, could do nothing with her boy Augustine. He ran around with a rough gang; sex fascinated him; and eventually, not bothering to get married first, he had a son to support. He decided to leave North Africa and teach school in Italy.

Between classes he did some sober thinking, desperate for a way out of the life of self-indulgence that curdled his soul with shame. In Milan he listened to Bishop Ambrose preach the message of Christ. He pondered and brooded. One day he heard a child singing in some sort of game, "Take up and read."

Augustine did pick up and read his New Testament, flipping it open to Romans 13:13–14. What would this passage mean to a guilt-ridden young man with Augustine's problem? Here are Augustine's own words describing the experience:

A fifth-century mosaic of Ambrose, from Milan, Italy

I snatched it [the New Testament] up, opened it and in silence read the passage upon which my eyes first fell: Not in rioting and drunkenness, not in chambering and impurities, not in contention and envy, but put ye on the Lord Jesus Christ and make not provision for the flesh in its concupiscences. *(Romans xiii:13) I had no wish to read further, and no need. For in that instant, with the very ending of the sentence, it was as though a light of utter confidence shone in all my heart, and all the darkness of uncertainty vanished away.*[3]

At last he had the answer. Bishop Ambrose baptized him as a Christian in the cathedral of Milan.

A sixth-century fresco of Augustine

Soon afterward his mother died; so did his young son. Back in Africa all alone, he decided to be a monk. But he was not to spend his days in a quiet monastery; in 395 he became bishop of Hippo.

Augustine found time in the midst of his new responsibilities to write down some of the most profound Christian thinking on record. As he watched barbarians plundering the Roman empire, he worked out theories to explain it all. These theories, written out in his book *The City of God*, gave medieval popes their grand vision of a Holy Roman Empire obedient to the voice of the church, proclaiming God's will.

For nearly sixteen hundred years Augustine's writings have challenged people to think. His life of soul-shaking ups and downs gave him some startling insights into the predicament of being human.

Mosaic of John Chrysostom   From the church of Saint Sophia, Istanbul, Turkey

THE UNPOPULAR GOLDEN-MOUTH

While Augustine was discovering what God does for us, John, Patriarch of Constantinople, was telling his fellow Christians what they must do for God. Can a minister preach a completely forthright sermon about Christian behavior without infuriating someone in the congregation? Patriarch John certainly did not succeed at it. He was drummed out of town for his preaching on Christian conduct and died in exile in A.D. 407. Later on, the fickle public decided that he had been a genius and started calling him Chrysostom (krĭs′ ŏs-tŭm), the Golden-mouthed.

Chrysostom preached first in Antioch where he told his prosperous parishioners to be concerned about the working conditions of the ships' crews who brought them their imported finery. He had much to say about how one should treat other members of one's family. His Antioch people loved him for his frankness.

But the emperor sent Chrysostom to Constantinople. There the pleasure-loving monks and priests resented his attempts to straighten them out. Wealthy ladies bridled at his remarks about the jewels they wore in a city where thousands starved. The empress was so furious that the emperor finally sent Chrysostom into exile. But the church ever since has been richer for Chrysostom's brave example of prophetic preaching.

23

If we had been Roman Christians after Augustine's time, we would have lived next door to terror, for imperial Rome lay in ruins at the feet of invading barbarians. What now would happen to the Christian church? Could it survive without Rome's strong arm to shield it? Would the invaders spare its monasteries? Would they listen to its missionaries? Would they bow the knee to its Lord?

Suppose missionaries had not gone seeking the Germanic tribesmen—would we now be Christians in the twentieth century?

MONASTICISM—OUT OF THIS WORLD

If you think it's hard to be Christian in our day and age, think how the Christian church had to struggle for a foothold in the wild and battle-scarred Europe after the fall of Rome. Thoughtful men asked, "Will the church be able to survive?" and "Will the church be able to remain truly *Christian*?"

It is an exciting pageant, this drama of a thousand years of church history—a pageant featuring barbarian hordes and Moslem horsemen, cloistered monks and crusading knights, Christlike saints and libertine popes. The light of faith illuminating this pageant flickered and flared in the fitful wind of medieval events. But always there were reverent and faithful hands to bear that torch into the future.

Rome fell, but the church stood. Why? The answer, in large part, was monasticism. The monastic system kept Christianity from being lost in the blood and thunder of Teutonic invasions. We can understand this more clearly if we look at the beginnings of Christian monasticism in the early centuries of the church.

24

A sixth-century
monastic prayer chapel,
County Kerry, Ireland

Christians did not invent the idea of going apart from the busy world of men to live alone in religious meditation. There had been Hindu hermits and Buddhist monks long before Jesus' day. John the Baptist was only one of many devout Jews who left the towns for the wilderness in a lonely search to know the will of God.

By the second century a number of Christians in Egypt were going off to live alone as hermits in the desert, meditating and trying to forget their physical bodies as completely as possible. But many of them discovered that complete solitude was hard on their sanity; they began to "see things," and Christian leaders started to question the wisdom of living entirely alone.

So it happened that Pachomius (pà-kō′ mǐ-ŭs) organized the first Christian monastery in the south of Egypt in A.D. 323 (just two years before the Council of Nicaea). His monks lived apart, away from the world of towns and trade, but they lived together, helping one another in their life of prayer and meditation. They engaged in physical work to keep their minds wholesome. Their daily program was carefully regulated by a set of rules. Pachomius' monastery proved so successful that several others were soon founded in Egypt.

The idea of monastic brotherhoods caught hold all through North Africa, Italy, Spain, and Gaul—in fact, throughout the Roman empire, even in faraway Ireland. When Rome crumbled, monastic brotherhoods survived outside the ravaged Roman towns.

Some of the monks worked quietly within the monastery walls copying Christian manuscripts. Others preached and taught the

A miniature manuscript illumination of the abbot of Monte Cassino with Benedict, founder of the monastery

people of nearby communities. Still other monks went farther out into the world, sometimes traveling in bands of twelve with a leader, as the twelve disciples had traveled with Jesus. These bands of missionary monks organized new churches and monasteries in the pagan wilderness of Europe.

One great monastery, Monte Cassino (mŏn'tē kȧ-sē'nō), stood out as a lighthouse in the troubled history of Europe. Built by an Italian monk named Benedict in 529, it stood high on a mountain where once a pagan temple had stood. Here Benedict developed a sound and sensible pattern for group living, the Benedictine Rule. He knew the value of hard labor in farm and workshop; he knew the value of prayer, study, and human fellowship. In the centuries that followed, new monasteries throughout Europe made use of Benedict's wise rule. Here is a brief excerpt from it:

We are, therefore, about to found a school of the Lord's service, . . . we shall run the way of God's commandments with expanded hearts and unspeakable sweetness of love; so that never departing from his guidance and persevering in the monastery in his doctrine till death, we may by patience share in the sufferings of Christ, and be found worthy to be coheirs with him of his Kingdom. . . .

Let not a free-born be preferred to a freedman, . . . for "whether bond or free," we are all one in Christ, and we all bear an equal burden of servitude under one Lord. . . .

Whenever any weighty matters are to be transacted in the monastery, let the Abbot call together the whole community, . . . all should be called for counsel, because the Lord often revealeth to the younger what is best. Let the brethren, however, give their advice with humble submission, . . . let all follow the Rule as their guide in everything, and let no one rashly depart from it.[4]

In these monasteries men were relatively safe from warfare, starvation, and worry. They could pray, they could study and copy books of Christian thought, they could teach their neighbors the Christian faith. Monasticism kept the church alive through the brutal centuries of barbarian invasions.

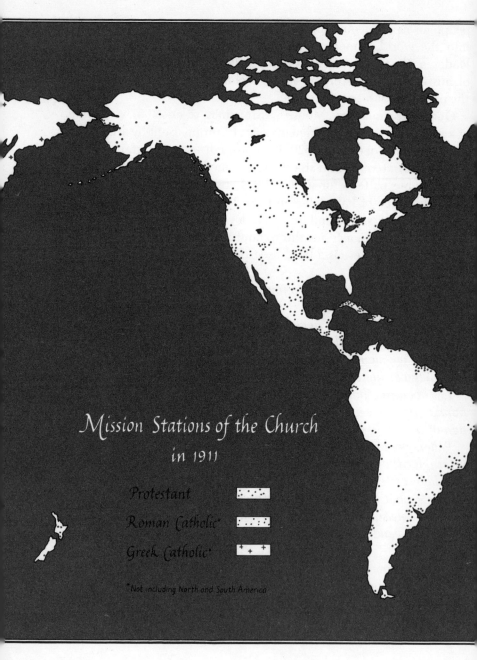

Mission Stations of the Church
in 1911

Protestant

Roman Catholic*

Greek Catholic*

*Not including North and South America

28

A seventh-century representation of a barbarian warrior

AN OAK TOPPLES IN GERMANY

Where were your ancestors twelve hundred years ago? Perhaps some of them were among the Germans who watched the stalwart Christian monk from England as he strode up to their sacred oak tree at Geismat in Hesse. Boniface (bän'ĭ-fās), so legend says, lifted his ax and swung it. Chips flew, and a sudden breeze made the leaves whir overhead. The oak groaned and fell, but the great god Thor did not arrive to smite Boniface with thunderbolts. Nor did the deity Woden (wō'd'n) intervene when Boniface cut the mighty oak into planks to build a Christian church. The Teutons of Hesse were convinced. They forsook Thor and Woden for Boniface's Christ.

Long before Boniface's time, the western half of the Roman empire had crumbled to dust under Gothic feet. The city of Rome had fallen into barbarian hands in 476. But the church survived the holocaust. Even before Rome fell Arian Christian teachings had spread among the invaders, who had a Visigothic translation of the Bible. Patrick had already planted the cross firmly on Irish soil, and the Frankish king, Clovis, had been baptized with three thousand of his people in 496. Although the empire fell, the church stood firm. In fact, without the Roman emperor to hold the reins, the church

A manuscript illumination showing a baptism and the martyrdom of Boniface

of western Europe came to have more influence on people's lives than had the church before the Roman empire fell.

Now, as ever, the people of Christ constituted a church on the move, a missionary church. From one country to another the flame of Christianity spread century after century. It swept into Scotland and England in the sixth century, and two hundred years later Boniface brought it to Germany.

The work was hard and it took time—more than a thousand years —to christianize all of Europe. Denmark saw no Christian missionary until 826, and the tenth century was nearly over before all of Scandinavia had forsaken the Norse gods in favor of Jesus Christ. By that time India had had a Nestorian Christian church for over six hundred years!

In those centuries of Christian expansion, the people of Christ found that their mission, as always, cost them something. While Boniface was holding a service along a Frisian river bank, marauders fell on the group and slaughtered everyone in their quest for loot. Boniface left a Christian Germany as his memorial; and his death, like that of Polycarp six centuries earlier in Smyrna, became a source of power in the fellowship of Christ's people. The mission was costly, but the church found glory in its cost. Out of death came resurrection.

In medieval Europe, we would have found the church anything but peaceful. Separated by political animosities and vast, bandit-infested wilderness, the eastern and western branches of the church developed many differences and finally severed relations in 1054. To increase his own political power, the western pope (Urban II) wanted a reconciliation with the eastern church. He saw his chance when Moslem invaders threatened the eastern church. "God wills it!" he cried, summoning western kings to battle the Moslems, but what would come out of the bloody crusading against the Moslems in the centuries that followed?

BEFORE IT WAS ISTANBUL

Have you ever visited an Eastern Orthodox church with its candles, its semi-Oriental music, its icons, and its incense? In many of their traditions, dating back to early days in Constantinople, the Eastern Orthodox churches differ from the Roman church, for the churches of the East became divided from Rome after northern invaders shattered Rome's might.

The popes of the western church took over some of the political power that western emperors had wielded before the invasions, but in Constantinople emperors continued to rule in vast power and splendor. Their word was law in the eastern church. The emperors were often generous overlords. Justinian, emperor in the sixth century, rebuilt Constantinople's beautiful church of St. Sophia. But the church of the East had to take orders as well as gifts from the emperors.

This manuscript illumination shows Emperor Leo ordering the destruction of an icon while the patriarch of Constantinople protests in vain

Sometimes imperial interference resulted in bloodshed. In 726 Emperor Leo sent his soldiers to remove statues of saints from the churches, stating that these statues were too much like pagan idols. When the soldiers started to take down a crucifix over the gate at Constantinople, a group of outraged ladies pulled the ladder out from under the soldiers, and they fell to their death. A riot followed. A century later, however, church and emperor agreed to permit the use of pictures and low-relief images to remind men of their beloved saints. You can still see similar images, or icons, in Orthodox churches today.

33

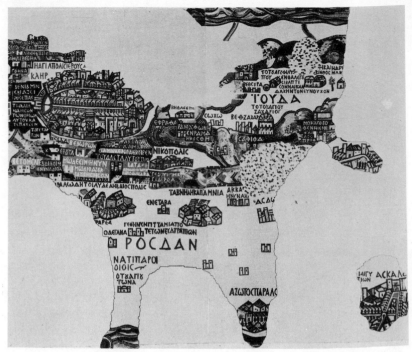

This sixth-century mosaic map of Jerusalem is part of the floor of the
Basilica of Madaba in Transjordan

Constantinople never governed so vast a realm of united believers as did the Roman church. The Moslem invasions of the
seventh century weakened the eastern church, perhaps the more
easily because Constantinople exercised no strong central control.
Each of the emerging nations of eastern Europe and the Middle
East eventually developed its own independent church, looking to
Constantinople only for spiritual guidance.

Rome and Constantinople continued to drift apart until the pope
and the Patriarch of Constantinople, jealous of each other's power,
excommunicated each other in 1054. This rift, although patched
up from time to time, has never healed. Will it heal in our time?
Many people think so. In 1964 the pope and the Patriarch of Constantinople met for the first time in over a thousand years. The
Eastern Orthodox churches also have strong ties of fellowship with
Protestantism.

This manuscript illumination from Madrid, Spain, shows crusaders attacking a Palestinian town

SHOULD URBAN HAVE DONE IT?

Rome had never seen such a peppery pope! Bishops and arch-bishops trembled when Urban II found them guilty of selling church offices or of getting involved with women. But Urban wasn't satisfied with reforming the church at home. He determined to organize a vast holy war against the Moslems who now ruled the land where Jesus had lived. Urban mustered support for this project through such fiery speeches as this one made to his bishops in Claremont in 1095:

You must carry succor to your brethren dwelling in the East, and needing your aid, which they have so often demanded. For the Turks, a Persian people, have attacked them . . . have already seven times . . . destroyed the churches and devastated the kingdom of God . . . the Lord prays and exhorts you, as heralds of Christ, by frequent exhortation, to urge men of all ranks, knights and foot-soldiers, rich and poor, to hasten to exterminate this vile race from the lands of our brethren . . . the sins of those who set out thither, if they lose their lives on the journey, by land or sea, or in fighting against the heathen, shall be remitted in that hour; this I grant to all who go, through the power of God vested in me. . . .

Let those who have formerly contended against their brothers and relatives now fight as they ought against the barbarians. . . . Let not those who are going delay their journey, but having arranged their affairs and collected the money necessary for their expenses, when the winter ends and the spring comes, let them with alacrity start on their journey under the guidance of the Lord.[5]

In response to Urban's summons, the warriors of all Europe joined to drive the Moslem Turks back from Constantinople and out of the Holy Land. When the crusaders finally captured Jerusalem, they celebrated with a gruesome massacre. In the name of the Prince of Peace blood was shed in brutal war.

In later crusades Christians lost Edessa, plundered Constantinople, surrendered Jerusalem, and tried in vain to get it back. Pre-teen boys set out on a children's crusade, only to end up in slave ships.

Why were Europe's men so hungry to fight in the burning dust of the Middle East? Part of the reason lay in the pope's promise that crusaders would receive complete forgiveness of sins (a plenary indulgence, it was called) for going on a crusade. The lure of wealth, glory, and fame played its part. So did the hope for excitement, and the opportunity to escape the narrow, boring routine of castle life.

For over two hundred years such hopes kept men slaughtering one another—until the last crusade fizzled out in 1329. When it was all over, what had been gained? Not the Holy Land—that would be in Moslem hands for nearly six more centuries. Instead of helping Constantinople, plundering crusaders had weakened it so badly it fell to the Moslems within a century, leaving a legacy of bitterness between the eastern and western churches.

But some progress did come. Crusaders returned to Europe aware of the great civilizations of Asia and with new ideas of art and medicine, philosophy and mathematics. No longer were men satisfied with the treadmill existence of village life. Merchants grew rich importing the Oriental fabrics and spices for which the wanderers had developed a liking. Italian cities, grown up overnight

A thirteenth-century French stained-glass medallion showing a scene from the crusades

as huge armies marched through, sent the pulse of trade far and wide. The crusades jostled Europe awake, ready for the Renaissance. The crusades and their aftermath also helped to produce the evils that reformers would condemn. But out of the crusades came also new insight and a mental alertness that were to help the reformers speak out against the sins of their church.

Would we have respected a church that produced lazy, immoral bishops, bloodthirsty knights who massacred Moslem children in Jerusalem, and great saints like Francis of Assisi? Would we have dreaded the church's threat of hellfire, or yearned for its promise of heaven? Would we have protested as we watched the church deteriorate among the luxuries of the Renaissance? Could we have hoped that real Christianity would somehow survive all the hollow ceremony and self-indulgence?

IF YOU HAD BEEN AROUND DURING THE CRUSADES

If you had been born in Europe in the late Middle Ages, you would have lived in a religious situation needing the changes that Luther and the other reformers would bring a few centuries later. Yet much would have been worth keeping. Let us look briefly at a few aspects of medieval Christianity.

Picture A. In the Middle Ages you would have believed in a very real devil who was trying to trick you into a hideous hell while the Virgin Mary and the saints encouraged you on the road to a glittering heaven. Even with their help, you would have expected a term in the fires of purgatory on the way.

Picture B. Your church would have been the social center of your village, with markets, plays, and other community events in the churchyard. But in the church could you really have found help in Christian living? Many priests were careless and corrupt; some hired other men to care for their parishes. Once in a while a reforming monk or bishop tried to set things straight in the midst of the widespread corruption.

Picture A. This fifteenth-century woodcut from a popular book entitled *The Art of Dying* shows devils at hand to receive the soul of the departed

Picture B. This manuscript illumination shows Lendit, an important medieval fair, held in the cathedral yard of a French town

39

Picture C. This fourteenth-century French manuscript illumination shows Christ and the horsemen of the Apocalypse in the garb of medieval knights

Picture C. Probably your ideas of Christian manhood would have centered in the ideal of a fighting knight or of a cloistered monk. You would have dedicated your weapons to God. Your church would have called for the Truce of God (halting battles from Wednesday evening until Monday morning) and the Peace of God (sparing priests, farmers, and other defenseless people), but loving your enemies, particularly the Moslem foe in the crusades, would have received little attention.

40

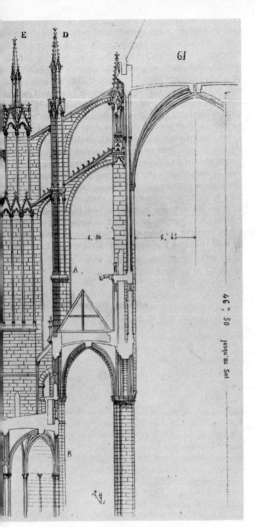

61

The Cathedral of Saint Maclou,
France

Picture D. A diagram of the flying buttresses
of Beauvais Cathedral, France

Picture D. You would have delighted in pilgrimages to the nearest cathedral—a mammoth soaring edifice of massive stone arches
and walls jeweled with windows of stained glass as glorious as your
notion of paradise. For generations all the Christians of your dio-
cese would have joined their labor and their gifts to build this
magnificent place of worship.

Picture E. A meeting of the one hundred clerks at the opening of
New College, Oxford, 1453

Picture E. If you had been bookish, perhaps your parents would
have sent you to one of the new church universities that had grown
out of the old cathedral schools. There you would have trained as
a priest, or even as a lawyer or physician. Although they were long
preoccupied with theology, these universities gradually became
centers for the exchange of new ideas on all sorts of subjects.

Picture F. Jan van Eyck's painting of Francis of Assisi receiving the Stigmata

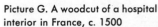

Picture G. A woodcut of a hospital interior in France, c. 1500

Picture F. You would have heard much about sinners—unworthy priests, brutal pirates and highwaymen, and ordinary folk who committed one or more of the seven deadly sins. But also you would have heard of saints—monks radiant with prayer, women who nursed their neighbors through plague, people whose goodness exceeded that of ordinary men. Such people, the church believed, had earned extra merit in the sight of God and so, after their death, could help other people toward a better understanding of the spirit of Jesus and toward greater ability to follow him. Saintly lives are among the greatest heritage the medieval church has given our world.

Picture G. You would have observed the hospitals for sick people, orphanages for children, and hospices for travelers maintained by your church. The church did care about people; at least the beginning of social service in Christ's name was present.

Picture H. Through the sale of indulgences, shown here in an illustration
from a sixteenth-century tract, high church officials wielded great power
over people and politics in the Middle Ages

Picture H. You would have been aware that the high dignitaries
of the church wielded great political power—more than any religious body holds in our times. The pope and his bishops had much
to say about political affairs in every country.

The Middle Ages contained many shadows—and much light.
How does this age compare with our own?

LITTLE BROTHER OF THE POOR

At a time when men's minds were full of the cruel pomp of the crusades, the most popular man-about-town in the Italian city of Assisi was doing some serious thinking about Jesus' call to loving service. Going with Francis on one of his escapades, you might not have guessed this, but his angry father sensed something different in Francis when he sold fabric from the family clothing store to rebuild a nearby church. And Francis began to help lepers who earlier had filled him with disgust. At mass one day in the little church he had rebuilt, Francis heard a priest reading the orders that Jesus had given his disciples and decided to follow them literally. He set out with no shoes, no money, and no extra clothing to preach the love of God in nearby towns and villages. (See Matthew 10:5–10.)

With his joyous, infectious spirit, Francis soon gathered around him a band of twelve "Little Brothers" pledged to poverty and chastity. They roamed as preachers from town to town. In 1210, Pope Innocent III gave them permission to found an order of traveling evangelists.

Francis expected his Little Brothers to remain faithful to Lady Poverty, following some trade or begging for bare necessities. But the Franciscans soon grew far too numerous for their humble, loving leader to control. Gradually they acquired lands and buildings and an organization much more complex than Francis wanted. The idealistic will he left for his order was bypassed. Yet few men have made a deeper mark on the world. This prayer of Francis' echoes his spirit.

O Lord, do thou so wean my mind from all that is under heaven by the fiery and sweet strength of thy love that I may be ready to die for the love of thy love as thou didst deign to die for the love of my love.

THE RENAISSANCE—EUROPE COMES BACK TO EARTH

Toward the end of the fifteenth century at about the time Columbus discovered America, a fiery Dominican monk named Savonarola (sà-vän-à-rō′là) was preaching terrifying sermons to the city of Florence. The Florentines had been enjoying Renaissance luxury, but now an invading French army knocked at the city gates. Savonarola thundered from the cathedral pulpit about the wrath of God kindled because of the people's love of finery. Their knees knocked. At carnival time they made a huge bonfire of their fine trinkets and paintings, and for a while Savonarola practically ruled the city.

But the earthy Renaissance pope, Alexander VI, talked the fickle Florentines into imprisoning their prophet. They tortured him, hanged him, burned his body, and threw it into the Arno River. Savonarola had made a brave try to purify the church and society, but he had pitted himself against the forces of the Renaissance that had awakened all Europe to the glories of life on this earth. Europe was in no mood to go back to contemplation of heaven and hell.

What was this Renaissance that had ridden into Europe on the heels of the last crusades? One way to find out is to look at the new paintings and statues—the work of Leonardo da Vinci, Titian, Michelangelo and others—that were moving Florentines and the rest of Europe to such enthusiasm. The people pictured in this art have nothing otherworldly about them. They do not look preoccupied with heaven and hell; they do not look as if they fasted painfully during Lent. They are handsome, healthy people dressed in princely outfits of silk, satin, velvet, fine linen, and wool, bordered in gold and silver, and highlighted by jewels. We see the lavish touch of the Orient in their costumes. In the buildings pictured behind these winsome figures, we see an echo of the pagan temples of Greece and Rome.

Europeans had been poring avidly over the pages of classical pre-Christian history. Scholars in the fourteenth and fifteenth centuries had rediscovered the joyous earthiness of Latin poets like Ovid and Horace. Classical art was newly appreciated. Even popes and archbishops were trying to live like Roman emperors.

Portrait of Savonarola by Bartolomeo
della Porta, San Marco, Florence

THE BIRTH OF VENUS   Botticelli
Savonarola denounced the Renaissance, here represented by the art of Botticelli, but the
forces of the Renaissance eventually silenced him in death

Telescopes and other scientific instruments as pictured in a book published in 1630

Along with poetry and art, the new interest in Greek and Roman culture had turned up fine traditions of democracy and justice, civic responsibility, and respect for law, all of which would enhance the ideas of the Christian society that were to develop in the New World in the coming centuries.

Science, too, formed part of the Renaissance picture. For the first time people dared to question what the church had declared about astronomy, geography, botany, zoology, and human anatomy. Gradually these brave scientists were bringing the universe into view and leading men toward a new appreciation for the creator God.

Humanist scholars in their new search of the classical languages —Greek, Hebrew, and Latin—blew the dust from ancient manuscripts of the Bible and of the Greek and Latin writings of the church fathers, unveiling them so they could once again enrich Christian minds.

Many things about the church of the Renaissance called for reform. After the dedicated, powerful popes of crusading days, the papacy went downhill. Self-indulgent popes let themselves be pushed around by ambitious kings. The French king even moved the pope to Avignon in 1309, and popes lived there for nearly seventy years of the so-called Babylonian captivity. They paid their bills by charging heavily for the services of the church and by exacting large fees from ambitious clergymen granted wealthy bishoprics.

The pope's critics often ended up at the stake. But criticism could hardly be kept down when papal politics became so corrupt that at one time three different people claimed to be pope—one at Avignon, one at Rome, and another who wanted Rome for himself. Archbishops and parish priests grew corrupt and careless under such leadership. The conflict of popes was finally settled by the Council of Constance in 1414.

But the Renaissance taught people that they could question the church when the church needed questioning. Earnest Christians looked longingly back to the purity and simplicity of the church of New Testament times. Reform was in the wind.

Though it was locked away under the load of medieval ritual, the Bible story of Christ's life, death, and resurrection still had great power to sway men's minds and hearts. What would happen when heroic souls determined to give the Bible back to the people? When they dared to measure church life and the conduct of the clergy by the yardstick of the Scriptures? If we had lived at the dawn of the Reformation, would we have found courage to side with these "heretics" who died at the stake?

UNDER ANATHEMA

When did the Reformation begin? Perhaps earlier than you think. By 1215, five years after Francis had received the pope's sanction for his little band of traveling preachers, another band of traveling preachers found itself under the official papal anathema. These men were exiled from the Roman church with a curse on their heads. Their crime was that they had translated the Bible into the language of the people to whom they preached, the people of southern France and of Lombardy in the mountains of northern Italy. For this crime, they were hounded by the watchdogs of the Inquisition for three long centuries. For this crime, they were heralded as the dawning lights of the Reformation. They were the Waldensians (wŏl-dĕn′sĭ-ŏnz), the Poor Men of Lyons and Lombardy, the followers of Peter Waldo.

Waldo, a wealthy merchant in Lyons, had given away all his goods in 1176 and had hired two priests to translate the New Testament for him into the language of the common people of his region.

A fourteenth-century manuscript illumination of an itinerant friar preaching out of doors.

He memorized a large portion of it and began his teaching and preaching. Soon he had disciples traveling two by two everywhere in the valleys of the Alps. The papal opposition only stiffened their determination to preach.

The Waldensians dared to speak out against the corrupt ways of the clergy. Even more important, they preached directly from the Bible, using translations in the people's everyday languages. Many of them learned whole books of the New Testament by heart. Waldensians said that prayers in Latin were useless, that sacraments administered by unworthy priests were invalid, that even laymen could hear confession, and that it was wrong to take oaths. They organized their own fellowship with clergy and bishops. When the Protestant Reformation began in Switzerland, the Waldensians became part of the Reformed movement. Some of them were later to join with descendants of John Huss's followers to form the Moravian fellowship.

Along with thousands like Francis within the church, the Waldensians and other critics of the church helped to pave the way for the Reformation by insisting that Christians must live Christian lives. They asserted that the good news in the Bible was more essential than the customs of the medieval church. Corruption must be done away with in the name of the Christ who stood forth in the pages of the Scriptures.

WYCLIFFE—ASHES IN THE AVON

Can you imagine risking death at the stake to translate the Bible into your own language? Men have taken that risk. Your right to read an English Bible was bought for you by men who died in flames more than five centuries ago.

A hundred years before Luther's birthday, John Wycliffe (wĭk'-lĭf) died in peace, but in 1414 the Council of Constance ordered his body dug up and burned, and his ashes thrown into the river Avon. If he had stayed quietly tending his parish at Lutterworth and lecturing at Oxford, this would not have happened to his bones, but neither would he have been called the morning star of the Reformation. Wycliffe could not keep quiet about the corruption he saw in his beloved church. Let the English lords take back their land from the soft and greedy clergy! Let them forbid the sending of English money to French popes at Avignon! Instead of tolerating corrupt popes and bishops, why not limit the clergy to priests and deacons responsible only to God?

Wycliffe chided the clergy in such words as these:

The office of curate [pastor] is ordained of God; few do it well and many full evil, . . . the curate that gives himself to study holy writ and teach his parishioners to save their souls, . . . is despised and persecuted by high priests and prelates. . . .

[Evil curates] waste poor men's goods on rich furs and costly clothes, and wordly [sic] array, feasts of rich men, and in gluttony, drunkenness, and lechery. For they sometimes pass great men in their gay furs and precious clothes—they have fat horses with gay saddles and bridles . . . .

Ye curates, see these heresies and blasphemies, . . . Forsake them for dread of hell, and turn to good life and true teaching of the gospel.[6]

Feeling that the people needed the Bible in their own language, Wycliffe worked out an English translation and sent out his Lollards (lŏl'ĕrdz), the "poor preachers," two by two to preach God's word across England. After Wycliffe's death public opinion turned against the Lollards, and many of them lost their lives at the stake.

> *The Avon to the Severn runs,*
> *And Severn to the sea;*
> *And Wycliffe's dust shall spread abroad*
> *Wide as the waters be.[6]*

HUSS—BONFIRE IN CONSTANCE

The same Council of Constance that ordered Wycliffe's bones dug up in 1414 also ordered his greatest disciple, John Huss (hŭs), burned at the stake. The emperor promised Huss safety if he would appear before the council, but he went back on his word. Here is part of a remarkable letter written by Huss as he waited for his sentence in the Constance prison:

I, John Huss, in hope servant of God, desire, that the believers in Bohemia who love the Lord, may live and die in grace, and at last obtain eternal life. . . .

I conjure you to beware of deceitful men, especially impious

53

The burning of Huss. From a fifteenth-century Czechoslovakian manuscript

priests, of whom the Lord has said, they are outwardly dressed in sheep's clothing, while within they are ravening wolves, ...

I write you this letter in my prison and with my fettered hand, expecting after tomorrow my sentence of death, and having an entire confidence in God that he will not forsake me.[6]

Huss was called on the carpet at Constance for preaching Wycliffe's ideas: do away with popes and bishops, indulgences, confession, pilgrimages, relics, and so on; give the common people communion wine as well as bread, and the Bible in their own language. Wycliffe's ideas had spread to Huss's homeland of Bohemia after Princess Anne of Bohemia married Richard II of England. At the University of Prague where Huss was teaching, he took up the challenge of Wycliffe's views, and many people backed him—partly to nettle the German churchmen oppressing Bohemia. It looked as if his reforms would stick.

But the thousands of church dignitaries who crowded into the city of Constance were determined to settle problems such as what to do with heretics like Huss. The council tried to burn up the teachings with the teacher. But ideas do not die as quickly as human bodies.

Though they disagreed and split into two camps, Huss's Bohemian followers remained loyal. Many eventually joined Luther's movement. Some started the Moravian fellowship that came later to Pennsylvania, bringing its wonderful hymns and its deep piety.

Richard Rolle of Hampole, an eminent English mystic. From a fourteenth-century manuscript

MYSTICS POINT THE WAY

While prophets like Wycliffe and Huss were crying out against the sins of the church, mystics like Gerhard Groote (gār′ärt grō′tĕ) were demonstrating that even in a wicked age men could live close to God. They also proclaimed long before the Reformation that a man's inner state of mind, rather than his outward deeds, witnessed to his relationship with God.

Gerhard Groote was a popular preacher and teacher in fourteenth-century Holland. In a corrupt age, he spoke out for a pure life lived close to God. He died while he was nursing plague victims during an epidemic, but his disciples went on to found a movement called the Brethren of the Common Life. They worked in the world, often as teachers, but lived a communal life like the early Christians, sharing all their property. Out of their fellowship came *The Imitation of Christ*, the classic devotional book attributed to Thomas a Kempis. In the centuries since it was written, many people have cherished it next to their Bibles. You will find a quotation from it on page 118.

Portrait of Erasmus by Holbein

REDISCOVERING THE SOURCES

The leaders of the Protestant Reformation did not think of their movement as new. They saw it rather as a return to the ways of the early church, a return to Christianity as it had been in the days of the apostles and the church fathers—Ignatius and Polycarp and the others. Many wanted to discard all the medieval superstitions, trappings, and rituals that had crept into the church.

Book-loving Renaissance humanists pioneered in this exploration of early Christianity. In the fifteenth and sixteenth centuries these men patiently studied, analyzed, translated, and published the ancient Greek and Hebrew texts of the Bible and the Greek and Latin writings of early Christian leaders. The new printing presses made copies of the work of these men available in the far corners of Europe. Thoughtful people everywhere were discussing the writings of early Christian leaders.

Many humanists allied themselves with the Protestant Reformation. Others preferred to watch from the sidelines, but the Reformation drew its strength from their work nonetheless. One who stayed on the Roman side and yet helped the Reformation was Erasmus (ĕ-răz'mŭs) of Rotterdam. An illegitimate child, he started out with very little money but managed to get a first-rate education. He spent his life traveling about Europe, tutoring, studying, and writing on current affairs. His book *In Praise of Folly* poked fun at the corrupt and stupid behavior of political rulers and officials in the Roman church. Erasmus prepared the original Greek New Testament for publication, with his own translation. He pleaded with people to read the Bible to learn what Jesus really had taught and how a Christian really should live.

Erasmus was vitally interested in the Reformation. He once stated that he had a Lutheran stomach: fish made him violently sick! But he hated to see the unity of the church destroyed, and felt that Luther was being too impetuous and outspoken in a situation calling for diplomacy. Here is a letter he wrote to Luther on this problem:

My dearest brother in Christ—
I have no words to tell you what a sensation your writings have caused here. It is impossible to eradicate from people's minds the utterly false suspicion that I have had a hand in them, and that I am the ringleader of this faction, as they call it. . . .

You have friends in England, and among them men of the greatest eminence, who think most highly of your writings. . . . For myself, I am keeping such powers as I have to help the cause of the revival of letters. And more, I think, is gained by politeness and moderation than by violence. . . . The violent wranglings in which some persons delight we can afford to despise.[7]

But Luther had decided that it was too late for diplomacy. For him the issues could not be compromised. The Reformation was on.

Luther, Zwingli, Calvin, the Anabaptists—these men built on the foundation that brave souls had been laying since Paul's day. Now they opened the Bible again and called all men to read it, each in his own language. They preached the message of salvation as God's gift received through sincere faith rather than earned by magic works. They demanded that the affairs of the church follow the New Testament pattern. How closely did these Reformation leaders agree with one another? How did they differ? What does our own congregation owe to each of them?

PROFESSOR FROM WITTENBERG

They must have looked at each other curiously, the newly-crowned, young Charles V of the Holy Roman Empire and the radical professor, Martin Luther, from Wittenberg. Enthroned at the imperial Diet at Worms (vôrms) in April of 1521, the young potentate ruled a domain that was bigger than anyone else's since Charlemagne's time. At this meeting of the Diet, Emperor Charles and the Diet were to judge a stalwart teacher in his late thirties who had been delivering dangerous opinions on religious matters. Luther had insisted that the pope and the great councils of the church could be mistaken, that only the Bible could be trusted absolutely as a guide for our lives, that no one could buy his way out of purgatory, and that monks and nuns should be allowed to marry. He claimed that all believers were priests to one another and that all lawful occupations served God. He asserted that fasting in Lent and other forms of self-punishment could not earn one salvation,

A sixteenth-century German woodcut of the Diet of Worms

nor could the saints help Christians win their way to heaven. Nothing would set man right with God except to trust in the power of the love of God in Jesus Christ to redeem one's life from sin.

How had Martin Luther come by such peculiar notions? His ideas were contrary to much that the church had taught for a thousand years. Was he a disciple of John Huss, the heretic burned at Constance? The Diet would decide his fate, it thought.

Luther had been brought up to fear God as a stern judge. The thought of God's anger at his sin so terrified him that he gave up the study of law to enter the Augustinian monastery at Erfurt. There he found out that no amount of monastic discipline or starving and whipping himself could assure him of God's forgiveness. He still knew he was guilty of sin. Only after he became professor of Bible in the new university at Wittenberg did he sense an answer to his terrible predicament. In preparing lectures on Paul's letter to the Romans, he gradually saw that man does not have to earn his salvation. Read Romans 3:21; 5:1 and 8; 6:23; and 10:9–10. Do you see what all this would have meant to Luther's discouraged, guilt-ridden soul?

This sixteenth-century woodcut shows John Tetzel selling indulgences. His activities especially ired Luther

In the words of Romans 5:1 Luther found the key to Christian freedom: "Since we are justified by faith, we have peace with God through our Lord Jesus Christ." Luther's Lord had died to save him; he was justified by his joyful faith. He was free to challenge the vast power of the church.

When the pope's representative came near Wittenberg selling indulgences to help pay for St. Peter's church in Rome, Luther wrote out ninety-five theses objecting to these indulgences and tacked up his arguments on Wittenberg's chapel door (the university bulletin board). He merely wanted to start a debate on the matter, but most Germans were fed up with the pope's abuses. Luther quickly found himself the leader of a vast movement to purify the church of false doctrine and corrupt practices. He based his attack squarely on scriptural authority, and his views swept the German nation. Even Wittenberg's Elector Frederick the Wise supported the rebel monk's party in an attempt to shake Roman controls off the German church.

Title page of the papal bull
excommunicating Luther, 1520

Pope Leo X became worried enough about Luther and his teach-ings to excommunicate him in a papal bull: Luther burned that document. Now here he was, called before the pope's political champion, Emperor Charles V, at the Diet of Worms.

"Here are the books you have written. Will you recant your words?" his critics demanded. Luther asked for time to think. Next day he made his famous answer:

My conscience has been taken captive by these words of God. I cannot revoke anything, nor do I wish to; since to go against one's conscience is neither safe nor right: here I stand, I cannot do other-wise. God help me. Amen.

Emperor Charles's Diet put Luther under the ban of the empire, giving him what amounted to a death sentence. As Luther traveled home from Worms, friends in the service of Elector Frederick am-bushed his party and carried him off to Wartburg castle, where he could live in safety disguised as a knight until things cooled off.

A woodcut of Luther translating the Bible. From a 1530 version of the German New Testament

In Wartburg Luther began a German translation of the Bible— so masterfully done that it helped to shape the German language. But some of his friends back at Wittenberg pushed reforms in undisciplined fashion by rioting in the churches. In spite of the ban, Luther returned to calm things down. He made many changes. He ended masses for the dead, urged that priests be paid from the civil treasury, substituted German for Latin in the church services, and encouraged monks and nuns to leave their monasteries. Luther himself married a nun. He wanted to reform the church, not leave it, but Rome would not accept Luther's reforms. So the split came, and much of northern Europe turned Lutheran.

BUSY, ACTIVE, MIGHTY

O it is a living, busy, active, mighty thing, this faith. It is impossible for it not to be doing good works incessantly. . . . This knowledge of and confidence in God's grace makes men glad and bold and happy in dealing with God and with all creatures. And this is the work which the Holy Spirit performs in faith. Because of it, without compulsion, a person is ready and glad to do good to everyone, to serve everyone, to suffer everything, out of love and praise to God who has shown him this grace.[8]

Thus does Luther describe the tremendous change that Paul's words in Romans worked in his heart.

Portrait of Ulrich Zwingli by Hans Asper

ZWINGLI OF ZURICH

Ulrich Zwingli (tsvĭng′lē), young priest at Einsiedeln in Switzerland, gazed long at the inscription over the Black Virgin's shrine: "Here is full remission of all sins, both from guilt and from punishment." And he thought to himself, "Rubbish!"

No one who knew Zwingli would have been surprised at the young man's reaction to the Black Virgin's promise. Born in 1484 among the Swiss mountains, he had always loved freedom. During his days as priest at Glarus, when he was twenty-two, he had protested the Swiss practice of hiring out as paid soldiers for other countries. He was known to hold humanist ideas, arrived at during student days in Switzerland and Vienna. Small wonder that the indulgences offered at the Einsiedeln shrine held no charm for him. In 1519 he left to preach in the city of Zurich.

Zurich rocked under the impact of Zwingli's lively sermons on Matthew. The people rallied to support him when he chased an indulgence-peddler back across the Alps toward Rome, and did away with lenten fasting and the intercession of the saints, with celibacy for the priesthood, and with church services in Latin.

Zwingli aimed to abolish everything in church practice that was not expressly commanded in the New Testament. He threw out the elaborate ritual of the mass and centered church services in study of the Bible. He read the New Testament in the Greek original as well as in the German spoken in Zurich. It was thrilling to hear the very Greek words that Paul had spoken. One worshiper said he felt as if he were being pulled up by the hair on his head!

The pope grew alarmed and urged Zurich to throw Zwingli out, but the town council stood solidly behind him. Zurich people loved Zwingli with a great loyalty. He was their brilliant young champion against the evils of the Roman hierarchy.

So successful was Zwingli in freeing Zurich's churches from Roman control that neighboring Catholic cantons feared that his movement would sweep through Switzerland, and they formed an alliance against him. A tragic war followed, and in the second engagement five hundred men of Zurich died in a single day. As Zwingli, their chaplain, stooped over a wounded soldier, a stone crashed against him and a lance struck him down.

"What evil is it?" he murmured. "They may kill the body but they cannot kill the soul."

MONSIEUR CALVIN COMES TO GENEVA

Devout church officials in France had their eyes on young John Calvin—disapproving eyes. Since his school days in Paris, Calvin had run around with a crowd of Protestants and humanists. In 1533 he became an avowed Protestant. When rumors reached him of plans to clamp down on French Protestants, Calvin knew very well that he was a marked man. Late in 1534 he walked out of Paris disguised as a peasant with a hoe over his shoulder and headed for Switzerland.

Switzerland was a good place for Protestants. Although the city of Zurich had lost its Zwingli in battle, it remained staunchly Protestant. Other reformers had gained a foothold in the French-speaking city of Geneva. By 1535 these reformers were influential enough to take over Geneva's churches, remove the images of saints, do away with mass, and chase the monks and nuns out of town.

Calvin found refuge in Protestant Basel, where in 1536 he published the first version of his famous *Institutes of the Christian Religion,* the most systematic presentation of Protestant principles to

An early portrait of John Calvin

that date. Refined and expanded many times, this monumental work shaped Protestant thought throughout Europe. When this young French Protestant journeyed to Geneva in 1536, the Genevans told him he was just the man to lead them in developing a sturdy Protestant church life. Calvin stayed in Geneva because he felt that "God had stretched forth his hand upon me from on high to arrest me." He worked in Geneva for the rest of his life, except for three years (1539–41) when he took refuge in Strassburg because of political opposition in Geneva.

Calvin found Geneva a corrupt city and went about setting things straight with a vigor sometimes frightening. By threats of jail sentences even for such things as sleeping in church and wearing too much jewelry, Calvin reformed the citizens of Geneva. He convinced the town council that its job was to enforce the teachings of the church; later on this arrangement would mark life in early New England.

Calvin organized the churches on a pattern called presbyterian, because decisions were made, not by bishops, but by laymen— presbyters or elders elected by each congregation to govern the church. Churches in a given region sent elders to meet together in a presbytery to decide questions affecting all churches of the area. This pattern of church government has been used by Reformed and Presbyterian churches to this day.

Calvin's theological teaching with its emphasis on the doctrine of double predestination may appear harsh by our standards. Here is how he stated his conviction a year after coming to Geneva:

> *The seed of the word of God takes root and brings forth fruit only in those whom the Lord, by his eternal election, has predestined to be children and heirs of the heavenly kingdom. To all others (who by the same counsel of God are rejected before the foundation of the world) the clear and evident preaching of truth can be nothing but an odor of death unto death. Now, why does the Lord use his mercy toward some and exercise the rigor of his judgment on the others? We have to leave the reason of this to be known by him alone. For, he, with a certainly excellent intention, has willed to keep it hidden from us all. The crudity of our mind could not indeed bear such a great clarity, nor our smallness comprehend such a great wisdom. . . . Only let us have this resolved in ourselves that the dispensation of the Lord, although hidden from us, is nevertheless holy and just. For, if he willed to ruin all mankind, he has the right to do it, and in those whom he rescues from perdition one can contemplate nothing but his sovereign goodness. We acknowledge, therefore, the elect to be recipients of his mercy (as truly they are) and the rejected to be recipients of his wrath, a wrath, however, which is nothing but just.*[9]

Despite his harshness we sense in all Calvin's writings, like the recurring theme of a symphony, the sturdy conviction of all genuine Christians that our lives must be obedient to the all-holy will of God. To Calvin's followers, predestination meant that *they* were

God's elect, his chosen ones, and that their lives *must* be holy. So sure were they of their own salvation that the Catholic inquisitors could not silence them. "God is sovereign and we are his elect," was their battle cry.

THE ANABAPTISTS GO ALL OUT

If you were to take seriously all the New Testament rules for holy living, would you make yourself conspicuous, reap criticism, spend time in jail? By trying to obey Jesus' commands literally, the strong-minded Anabaptists (that is, re-baptizers) let themselves in for much worse punishment during Reformation days.

Since the New Testament said nothing about baptizing babies, Anabaptists refused to baptize children too young to understand the Christian faith. Believing that their own babyhood baptism had been no true baptism, they baptized each other anew. Many were punished for this by drowning—a horrible joke of a baptism.

The magistrates were angry at more than the re-baptizing. Anabaptists said that Jesus opposed the taking of oaths, even in law courts. They refused to share in warfare or in capital punishment of criminals, believing that God forbids killing our fellowmen. (Today there are people in most Protestant denominations who agree.) Because the government was involved in soldiering and capital punishment, Anabaptists said Christians should not take public office. Anabaptists also believed in a "gathered" church, consisting only of baptized believers, not of the community at large.

These ideas shocked other Protestants, as well as Catholics. Magistrates burned alive several of the Anabaptist ringleaders, drowned many others, and exiled or jailed hundreds, all of whom counted it a privilege to suffer for their Lord. The survivors were driven from country to country, until many finally found refuge in Holland. They continued quietly and steadfastly to obey Jesus as they understood him. Their ideas spread over Europe and England and to the New World where their spiritual descendants today include Baptists, Quakers, Brethren, Amish, and many other groups that enrich and strengthen the religious fiber of our nation.

An engraving showing Protestants destroying statues and religious objects in their zeal for reform

WHY THE REFORMATION?

Luther did not split the church. Neither did Zwingli nor Calvin. When these reformers came along, the church was already suffering from decay. The challenge of the reformers merely unveiled the corruption. What had predisposed people to turn their backs on the vast organization that for more than a thousand years had controlled men's lives in western Europe?

1. *New ideas undermined old dogmas.* Fermenting in men's minds was a whole new world of insights brought to Europe by crusaders returning from the Middle East and by refugee scholars driven out of Constantinople in 1453. Many Italian humanists laughed at the church's dogmas as they read the poetry and philosophy of ancient Greece and Rome.

2. *Immorality rotted the church's fabric.* Many high church officials reveled in Renaissance luxury and corruption.

3. *Nations grew powerful.* Kings had overcome the power of feudal lords and they yearned to stop the pope's interference in national affairs. Their people began to think of themselves first as Englishmen or Frenchmen or Germans.

This German picture of a Venetian shipyard shows how ships were built to carry explorers and merchants around the world in the late fifteenth century

4. *People were on the move.* Men could now leave their native villages for the newly-developed towns and cities and enter the exciting world of commerce. As the horizons of men's lives were pushed back, the church lost its standing as the center of village life.

5. *Humanists rediscovered early Christianity.* Scholars reading the writings of the early church fathers discovered that the early church had taught a faith without the elaborate ritual now associated with worship.

6. *Many reforms were already in the air.* In the two hundred years before Luther's time, courageous leaders had rediscovered the essence of the New Testament faith. They had condemned the corrupt lives of some of the clergy, had translated the Bible into everyday languages, and had urged lay people to read it. They had defied popes and councils in the name of scriptural authority. Their seed was now bearing fruit.

7. *The right men spoke up at the right time.* Martin Luther, Ulrich Zwingli, John Calvin, and the others did not create the Reformation by themselves. But they had eyes to see the need for it, courage to speak out for it, and wisdom to steer it into fruitful and enduring channels.

When the tide of the Reformation washed over England, the thundering waters rolled and boiled as men fought out the vital issues. Was England's religion to be the home-ruled Catholicism of Henry VIII? The Romanism of Bloody Mary? The gay Protestantism of Elizabeth and James and Charles? The sober, anticeremonial religion of the Puritans? The exclusivism of the independent, gathered churches of the first Congregationalists? How did each of these groups influence the church life we know today?

BE OF GOOD COMFORT, MASTER RIDLEY

If your ancestors were British, they probably spent many sleepless nights during the blood-and-thunder decades of England's Reformation.

The Reformation in England was a jumbled mixture of cheap politics and heroic glory. It officially began when a tyrannical king divorced one of his six successive wives. But the Reformation spirit was too noble to be chained to the whims of a tyrant. The drama moved on to such poignant scenes as the death of two English Protestant bishops, chained together at one stake during the reign of Catholic Bloody Mary. "Be of good comfort, Master Ridley," said the fearless Reformation preacher, Hugh Latimer, to the bishop of London before their death. "Play the man. We shall this day light such a candle by God's grace in England as I trust shall never be put out."

England had long complained about the pope's interference in English affairs and his demands for English money. But Henry

Engraving after a portait of
Nicholas Ridley

Engraving after a portrait of
Hugh Latimer

VIII brought things to a head when Pope Clement VII refused him a divorce from his queen, Catherine of Aragon. By 1533 Henry had declared himself head of England's church and appointed an archbishop who gave him his divorce. Though he had ruthlessly suppressed the new Lutheran ideas in England, Henry now closed nearly four hundred monasteries and ordered English Bible reading for all churches.

During the short reign of Henry's son, Edward VI (1547–1553), the Church of England did away with saints' statues and allowed priests to marry. Archbishop Cranmer prepared an English Book of Common Prayer that has enriched the worship of English-speaking Protestants ever since. When sickly young Edward died, his Catholic half-sister, "Bloody Mary," came to the throne. In her five-year reign she tried to return England to the Roman Catholic fold. Many Protestants were killed in her persecutions.

Her successor, Elizabeth, had been reared a Protestant and restored the practices of Edward's reign. She steered a skillful middle course between Catholicism and the extreme Protestantism of the Puritans. The *Thirty-Nine Articles of Religion* were passed by Parliament in her reign and remain today as the tenets of the Church of England.

This "Hieroglyphic of Britain" symbolizes the emerging supremacy of British naval power in the time of Elizabeth I

PURITANS TACKLE ENGLAND

One Sunday morning toward the middle of the seventeenth century, a doughty little woman in Edinburgh threw her three-legged stool at her clergyman, screaming, "Will ye say mass in *my* ear?"

Whatever was her trouble? Her trouble was a sturdy Puritan streak that wouldn't let her be still when England sent this rector in his robes to read "popish ritual" to her out of a prayerbook. She was demanding a religion of the heart, and she distrusted ritual and ceremony.

We first hear about the Puritans after Queen Elizabeth came to the throne in 1558. She had made England Protestant again after the reign of her Catholic half-sister, Mary, but the Puritans felt that the English church still reflected too many of the old Catholic ways. Some of the Puritans had hidden from Mary in the Swiss Protestant cities and wanted to see England as sober, righteous, and godly as Zurich and Geneva. They demanded better preaching, higher moral standards among the clergy, and God-centered holidays (no tippling or cavorting). They objected to statues of saints, to kneeling at communion (the bread is not physically Christ's body, they said), and even to wedding rings—too popish! Their protest had its roots in their concern for a deep piety of the heart, a piety that needed no elaborate ritual.

Gay, extravagant Elizabethans had no stomach for such opinions and tried to suppress them. But the Puritans were too earnest to be silenced by Elizabeth's edicts against their prophesyings.

When James I came to the throne in 1603, the Puritans asked him to make the Church of England more like the Scotch Presbyterian church. They regarded the Presbyterian system with elders and ministers elected by the congregation as more in keeping with God's will than the English system of bishops and archbishops inherited from Catholicism.

James, however, suspected that the democratic presbyterian system would undermine his power. All he did for the Puritans was to order a new translation of the Bible—the King James Version. When James's high-living son, Charles I, took over, the Puritans' patience gave out. They called on Scotland's armies to help them control England. War broke out, and King Charles and Archbishop Laud lost their heads. England became a kingless commonwealth ruled by the Puritan Lord Protector, Oliver Cromwell.

But by 1660 after the death of Cromwell, the English people were tired of the strict Puritan rule. They brought Charles II, son of their beheaded king, to the throne. Persecution came again to the Puritans who could not go along with the ways of the Church of England. Several spent years in jail; some were even martyred before England finally passed an Edict of Toleration in 1689.

FROM A PURITAN DIARY

Puritans protested against the external ceremony of the Church of England because they stood for a religion of the spirit to which such externals were hindrances, not helps. These words of John Winthrop in his *Christian Experiencia*, written in 1628, illustrate well his concern for inner communion with Christ:

> *Now could my soule close with Christ, and rest there with sweet content, so ravished with his love as I desired nothing nor feared anything, but was filled with joy unspeakable, and glorious with a spirit of adoption. . . . The unspeakable comfort that I had in the . . . sweet communion with my Lord Jesus Christe filled me with such joye, peace, assurance, boldness, etc. . . . But the greatest of all was the assurance he gave me of my salvation, and grace over some corruptions which had gotten masterye of me.* [10]

74

A little group of hunted Londoners in the year 1571 protested in sorrowful anger over the death of their minister, Richard Fitz, "by long imprisonment pined and killed." They declared that "though we should cease to groan and cry unto our God to redress such wrongs and cruel handlings of his poor members, the very walls of the prisons about this city . . . would testify God's anger kindled against this land for such injustice and subtle persecution." [spelling modernized] [11]

In a day when independent church meetings were considered treason against Queen Elizabeth and her Church of England, Richard Fitz had led his little band to form one of the first Congregational churches in English history. As their defiant covenant explained, they were shaking the dust of the Anglican church off their feet. Most Puritans were willing to remain as critical members of the Church of England, but Fitz's group had decided to meet outside the established church. This was a bold step, and Fitz paid the ultimate price for it.

Another courageous Separatist leader, Robert Browne, organized a Congregational church in Norwich in 1581 and was jailed thirty-two times. Later, hiding in Holland, he wrote his famous *Treatise of Reformation Without Tarrying for Anie.*

The Separatists stood for an idea that has become one of the keynotes of our Protestant way of worship in America. They held that a church should be a "gathered" fellowship of believing Christians, rather than a collection of everyone living in the neighborhood, or parish, to use the old Catholic term. The church should consist only of those who had really experienced Christ's salvation and had chosen to bind themselves to Christ and to one another in a covenant.

Although long-suffering Robert Browne finally went back to the Church of England, many of his followers held out for their independent church life, even crossing the North Sea to Holland in order to worship in freedom. To these Congregational voyagers New England owes its beginnings. They were the pilgrim fathers.

Now the story moves to the New World, as harried Separatists and other Puritans found refuge there from English oppression. What sort of life did they build for themselves on the shores of Massachusetts? What aspects of their religion are valid for our lives? How did their pioneering affect the nation we live in today? In what respects have we grown beyond their limitations?

A BON VOYAGE PARTY MARKS BRAVE BEGINNINGS

The year 1620 saw a fateful farewell party at Pastor John Robinson's big house in the Dutch city of Leyden. It celebrated the beginning of a new experiment for the human race. As members of the congregation gathered to eat a last meal together and sing their beloved psalms, they must have wrestled with the pain of parting. One hundred two of their number would sail for the New World to follow their Separatist faith under the English flag, while the majority would stay behind with their pastor in Holland. Both stay-at-homes and voyagers would remember Robinson's tender good-by, his confidence "that the Lord had more truth and light to break forth out of his holy word."

Such faith would be sorely needed during the pilgrims' first winter in the New World. William Bradford, governor of Plymouth, gives us an eyewitness account of those first months:

Being thus passed the vast ocean, and a sea of troubles before in their preparation ... they had now no friends to welcome them nor inns to entertain or refresh their weatherbeaten bodies; ... the whole country, full of woods and thickets, represented a wild and

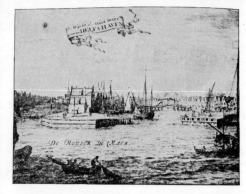

An engraving of the dock at Delfthaven, Holland, where the Pilgrims took ship on the first leg of their journey to the New World

savage hue. If they looked behind them, there was the mighty ocean which they had passed and was now as a main bar and gulf to separate them from all the civil parts of the world. . . .

In two or three months' time half of their company died, especially in January and February, being the depth of winter, and wanting houses and other comforts; . . . So as these died some times two or three of a day . . . there was but six or seven sound persons who to their great commendations, be it spoken, spared no pains night nor day, but with abundance of toil and hazard of their own health, fetched them wood, made them fires, dressed them meat, made their beds, washed their loathsome clothes, clothed and unclothed them. In a word, did all the homely and necessary offices for them which dainty and queasy stomachs cannot endure to hear named; . . . Two of these seven were Mr. William Brewster, their reverend Elder, and Myles Standish, their Captain . . . the Lord so upheld these persons as in this general calamity they were not at all infected either with sickness or lameness.[12]

MASSACHUSETTS BAY GETS GOING

When the Plymouth Separatists had been farming a little over eight years, they received a call for help from John Endicott, leader of a band of Puritans settling in at Salem up the coast. Plymouth sent Dr. Fuller to cure Endicott of scurvy and to persuade him to organize the Salem church along Congregational lines. Thus began a fellowship between the Plymouth people and the thousands of Puritans who would be settling the Boston area, shouldered out of England by King Charles's oppression.

The Puritans started little churches wherever they settled. The preachers thought of themselves as clergymen of the Church of England; but without bishops around, they could organize their churches by the simple New Testament pattern of local autonomy that was already being tested at Plymouth. The members of each new congregation drew up and signed their names to a covenant for their church. The covenant of the Salem Church, drawn up in 1629 reads as follows.

We covenant with the Lord and one with another and doe bynd our selves in the presence of God, to walke together in all his waies, according as he is pleased to reveale himself unto us in his blessed word of truth.

For six years the Puritans around Boston built homes and churches. In 1636 they decided to start a college where future ministers could be trained—so began Harvard University.

Ten years later the first big neighborhood assembly of Congregational leaders was held, the Cambridge Synod. This gathering of churches worked out the principles that would govern their fellowship of churches. Many of those principles still guide churches of Congregational background today.

Here are the requirements for church membership that delegates to the Synod wrote into their *Cambridge Platform* in 1648:

A personal & public confession, & declaring of God's manner of working upon the soul, is both lawful, expedient, & useful. . . .
The like trial is to be required from such members of the church, as were born in the same, or received their membership, & were baptized in their infancy, or minority, by virtue of the covenant of their parents, when being grown up into years of discretion they shall desire to be made partakers of the Lord's supper: . . . therefore it is requisite that these as well as others, should come to their trial & examination, & manifest their faith & repentance by an open profession thereof, before they are received to the Lord's supper, & otherwise not to be admitted there unto.

A STERN AND ROCKBOUND FAITH

The Calvinist doctrine that had brought Puritans across the Atlantic was a severe faith, impressive in its emphasis on God's power and on the majesty of God's holy will. It was so preoccupied with the power of God that it had little to say about the forgiving, fatherly love of God.

A poet with the interesting name of Michael Wigglesworth celebrated the Calvinist mood in a long poem called "The Day of Doom," published in 1662. It described the last judgment and for a hundred years was probably the most popular poem in America. Puritan children had to memorize it along with their Scriptures. Here is a sample of Wigglesworth:

> Mean men lament, great men do rent
>   their robes, and tear their hair:
> They do not spare their flesh to tear
>   through horrible despair.
> All kindreds wail: all hearts do fail:
>   horror the world doth fill
> With weeping eyes, and loud outcries,
>   yet knows not how to kill.
>
> *   *   *
>
> They wring their hands, their caitiff-hands
>   and gnash their teeth for terror;
> They cry, they roar for anguish sore,
>   and gnaw their tongues for horror.
> But get away without delay,
>   Christ pities not your cry:
> Depart to Hell, there may you yell
>   and roar eternally.

Can you imagine what it must have been like for Puritan youngsters to brood over the terror of this picture? They truly believed that they could do nothing to deserve salvation from Wigglesworth's hell. Only God could save them, if God so chose. No wonder sensitive souls often went frantic with worry.

T H E
BLOVDY TENENT,
of PERSECUTION, for caule of
CONSCIENCE, difcufled, in

A Conférence *betweene*
TRVTH and PEACE.

VVHO,
In all tender Affeċtion, prefent to the High
Court of *Parliament*, (as the *Refuli* of
their *Difcourfe*) thefe, (amongft other
Paffages) of *higheft confideration.*

Printed in the Year 1644.

Title page of the 1644 issue of *The Bloody Tenent*
by Roger Williams

ROGER WILLIAMS OPENS A DOOR

Not by accident are you today free to join the United Church of
Christ or the Presbyterian, Lutheran, or Episcopalian churches, or
the Zen Buddhists if you want. A long line of heroic people paid
heavily to free your religious life from government control.

America's most famous example is Roger Williams who founded
Rhode Island. This London tailor's son had studied for the ministry

at Cambridge University; later he came to New England to serve churches near Boston. But the Massachusetts authorities objected to his ideas. Williams insisted that the civil government should not dictate to its people in matters of religion. In his *The Bloody Tenent of Persecution* he tells us what he thought of governments that tried to force people into one brand of religion or another. Here is a sample of *The Bloody Tenent:*

What fearful cries within these twenty years of hundred thousands men, women, children, fathers, mothers, husbands, wives, brethren, sisters, old and young, high and low, plundered, ravished, slaughtered, murdered, famished! And hence these cries, because men fling away the spiritual sword and spiritual artillery (in spiritual and religious causes) and rather trust for the suppressing of each other's God, conscience and religion (as they suppose) to an arm of flesh and sword of steel. . . .

Such persons only break the cities' and kingdoms' peace, who cry out for prisons and swords against such who cross their judgment or practise in religion. . . .

Is not this to take Christ Jesus, and make him a temporal king by force? [6]

Roger Williams' viewpoint conflicted with the views of Massachusetts' civic leaders. Their Puritan towns permitted no one to vote in town meetings except church members. Baptists were discriminated against and Quakers were suspected of being in league with the devil. Four of them would be hanged in Boston in 1659–1660. Massachusetts had not yet learned that religious freedom was for everybody.

The Massachusetts General Court ordered Williams out in the middle of the winter of 1636. He went south to found Providence, which became a refuge for all victims of religious persecution. Williams was baptized by one of the Anabaptists who took shelter at Providence, but he spent the latter years of his life as a "seeker," not a member of any church. His courage gave all of us a charter to seek God for ourselves without government coercion.

Our church-minded ancestors in pre-Revolutionary America agreed on one thing: religion was terribly important. But they disagreed violently as to the proper temperature of religious experience. Where would we have stood? Would we have favored the passionate revivalistic oratory of the Rev. Mr. Jonathan Edwards? Or would the cool, reasonable approach of preachers in the coastal cities have suited us better? Would we have liked the warm piety of the German Reformed newcomers down near Philadelphia? Each of these groups wove its colorful strand into the religious fabric of the new nation.

FIREWORKS IN NORTHAMPTON

In a quiet, backwoods community like Northampton, Massachusetts, around 1735, life would have been pretty dull. Indian raids were mostly a thing of the past, and the excitement of the coastal towns was out of reach. There was plenty of time to get into trouble and to search one's soul afterwards.

Northampton's most dramatic attraction was the brilliant, fiery young Congregational preacher Jonathan Edwards. He spoke electrically on the majesty of God and the fearfulness of hell. He pleaded with his people to repent of their sins and accept God's salvation, to live on a higher plane as befitted those who were the Lord's elect.

Quite suddenly he began to get results. One of Northampton's gayest young ladies repented and joined the church. Soon others were flocking in. It took Edwards only six months to swell the

Portrait of Jonathan Edwards
by Joseph Badger

church roll by three hundred. The movement continued until it
included practically everyone in Northampton.

After nearly all souls were gathered into the church, boredom
evidently set in. Several of the younger set were caught giggling
over a book on midwifery and Edwards disciplined with a heavy
hand. There were suicides attributed to religious brooding. In 1750
the congregation voted by an overwhelming majority to ask Jonathan Edwards to leave.

The rest of his story is rather short and sad. He took the dismissal
with Christian grace and went to Stockbridge to write books and
preach to the Indians. He spent his last few months as president of
Princeton and died in 1758 of a bungled smallpox vaccination.

But this movement was to sweep America. The eloquent George
Whitefield preached salvation up and down the colonies, and Congregationalists and Presbyterians everywhere divided into two
camps. The New Lights, builders of Princeton College, were on fire
for the revival preaching that brought such amazing results; but
the Old Lights, with Harvard and Yale as their strongholds, deeply
distrusted such emotion-packed methods.

CATECHIZATIE, OVER DEN
Heidelberghschen
CATECHISMUS.
door PETRUM DE WITTE

tUtrecht By DE WEDUWE POOLSUM 1705.

Title page of a Dutch edition of the Heidelberg Catechism

Watercolor by Lewis Miller of a Lutheran schoolroom in York, Pa., in 1805. Similar schoolrooms had existed in the Pennsylvania wilderness for more than fifty years

PASTOR SCHLATTER LOOKS BACK

Michael Schlatter (shlăt'ĕr) developed an odd habit in his later years. Coming in from the road with dust on his spectacles, he would begin his hurried walk up the aisle of his Barren Hill church in Pennsylvania between rows of sturdy farmers with their neatly-aproned wives. Halfway to the pulpit, Pastor Schlatter would halt, pull his spectacles off his nose, and snatch up a corner of one of those pretty aprons to wipe his glasses clean.

But nobody minded. Schlatter had ridden faithfully for many years over the rough hill paths to visit his hard-working German parishioners at their cabin firesides. He had such interesting stories to tell about the days when the German Reformed people were new in Pennsylvania.

"Why did they come?" a youngster might ask the pastor, and he would reply, "Well, things were going badly for the German Reformed people in the Palatine country along the Rhine toward the end of the 1600's. Louis XIV of France burned hundreds of towns and villages; his armies scourged the area until people were ragged and hollow-eyed. Their French Catholic overlords locked them out of their Reformed churches.

"Many of these beleaguered Germans headed for the New World early in the 1700's. Some of them settled in New York, a few went to the Carolinas, but most came with their Bibles and their Heidelberg Catechisms here to Pennsylvania where the Quakers wel-

Lithograph of the Moravian settlement at Bethlehem, Pa., in 1757

comed them. Philadelphia was already full of the English, so the newcomers began clearing wilderness to the north and west. They depended on their schoolmasters to lead worship services and to teach religion to their children. But for communion or for baptism of their babies they had to trek to Philadelphia to the Presbyterian pastors, whose English they couldn't understand."

"Was that before schoolmaster Boehme (bām) was ordained?" the boy might inquire.

"Yes, John Philip Boehme helped to solve the problem by persuading the Dutch Reformed ministers up in New York to ordain him. Pastor Boehme organized three little congregations north of Philadelphia in 1725 and served them communion. More ministers came to help, more churches were organized, and more Reformed people crossed over from the Palatinate. By 1730, over half the Germans in Pennsylvania were Reformed."

"You came over in 1746, didn't you, Pastor Schlatter?"

"Yes, the Dutch Reformed church paid my way across so I could help Pastor Boehme. I remember riding out with Boehme and Pastor Weiss (wīs), soon after I landed, to visit the Tulpehocken (tūl-pĕ-hŏk'ĕn) Church. The people wept; they told us that not since they left the fatherland had they seen three preachers together in one church! The next spring at Fredericktown, I served communion in a new church that wasn't yet finished. The good people looked at me and at the baptismal water and the communion elements there on the table in front of me, and the tears rolled down their cheeks. How many years had it been since they'd watched a baby baptized or shared in the Lord's supper? I fell on my knees and prayed God's blessing on the dear people and their new church." [13]

Following the American Revolution in 1793, three years after Pastor Schlatter's death, the German Reformed people felt they should go their own way independent of the help for which they had looked to the Dutch Reformed Church. So they turned their coetus (kō-ē'tŭs), the annual assembly of ministers and elders, into a self-governing synod. By that time there were 178 congregations. The first chapter was over; they were on their way.

Drawing of the Falkner Swamp Church, north of Philadelphia, where schoolmaster Boehme first served communion in 1725

The Old Brick Church (St. Luke's Church), near the site of the Jamestown settlement in Virginia, is the oldest Protestant house of worship in America. It is usually dated 1632

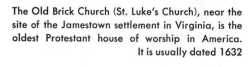

Drawing of the Quaker Meeting House, Flushing, N.Y., built in 1694

Woodcut of the Old Meeting House in Hingham, Mass., built in 1681. The wood of the frame is from the meetinghouse, as is the nail in the lower right-hand corner of the frame

YANKEE RELIGION

If after the Revolutionary War you had been a Yankee peddler hawking your wares through the brand-new United States, what would you have noticed about religion in your young country?

You might have observed that most people did not bother about religion in any formal way; the majority were not church members. But you would have seen that the churches and their pastors wielded powerful influence in their communities. Especially in New England they had led in shaking off British control and were now helping to shape government, education, and many other aspects of the life of the new nation.

You would have found the Congregational churches state-supported in most of New England, but making room for Baptists, Quakers, Presbyterians, and several other groups. All through New York, New Jersey, and Pennsylvania you would have met the German Reformed people along with Amish, Mennonite, Lutheran, and many other German groups, now far outnumbering the Quakers who had started Penn's Woods. In New York State you would have observed a strong Dutch Reformed group, and you would have found Presbyterians in all the central states.

You would have seen Methodist circuit riders gathering their flocks in the central and southern Atlantic states. In the older seaboard towns the Anglican church would be flourishing under a new American name, Protestant Episcopal, while Baptist congregations thrived in the pioneer settlements farther west.

This kaleidoscope of churches would be producing lively religious arguments for you to ponder while you rode along, as others pondered under Harvard elms or before cabin fireplaces. The Christian faith was a very live issue. As the fledgling nation moved toward maturity, more and more people would be flocking into its growing churches.

Jonathan Edwards' crusade in Massachusetts was part of a vast movement of religious feeling. In England this upsurgence centered in John Wesley and his co-workers as they launched Methodism. Would we have joined the mobs that stoned those soapbox orators, or would we have sensed in Wesley's preaching the beginning of something tremendous—a fire that would sweep around the world with the missionaries of the nineteenth century?

"MY HEART STRANGELY WARMED"

It was a rather shocking thing his mother was doing, John knew, conducting religious gatherings outside of church and doing the speaking herself as if she were an ordained minister instead of a mere woman. Susannah Wesley, wife of the rector in Epworth, England, presumed to hold meetings in her parsonage kitchen on Sunday afternoons. But to nine-year-old John, his mother's Sunday talks were fascinating windows to adventure. She told her little audience —her houseful of children, her servants, and some interested neighbors—about the hardships and triumphs of two German missionaries —Ziegenbalg (zē'gĕn-bälg) and Plutschau (plĭt'show)—who had gone to India in 1706. What discomforts those two had suffered under India's fierce sun! But they carried with them a stronger warmth, the fire of German pietism. How much did young John understand of this warmth that was spreading through Germany, this new love for Christ, and this fervor to serve him? Now for the first time this love had sent Protestants into Asia with the good news of Jesus. How far would that love send John Wesley when he became a man?

An engraving from a picture of
John Wesley by William Hamilton

A nineteenth-century engraving of a camp meeting on the American frontier.
Methodist circuit riders conducted many such meetings

Years later other German pietists were to help John find his
answer. On his way to missionary work in Georgia in 1735 he
learned to know the deep faith of German Moravians who were
crossing on his ship, and he pondered this faith wistfully.

The failure of his work in Georgia discouraged him deeply. He returned to England determined to learn more about the religious vitality he had sensed among the Moravians. Wesley did renew his acquaintance with the Moravians and subsequently experienced the turning point in his life and faith. Here is his own description of the experience:

In the evening I went very unwillingly to a society in Aldersgate Street, where one was reading Luther's preface to the Epistle to the Romans. *About a quarter before nine, while he [Luther] was describing the change which God works in the heart through faith in Christ, I felt my heart strangely warmed. I felt I did trust in Christ, Christ alone for my salvation; and an assurance was given me that he had taken away* my *sins, even* mine, *and saved* me *from the law of sin and of death.*[6]

As a result of this experience John Wesley traveled up and down England, usually on horseback or on foot, preaching in fields or marketplaces to the farmers, laborers, and miners who were not welcome in the sanctuaries of the aristocratic Church of England. The lords and ladies of the land did not want these dirty people pressing near to spoil their fine clothes when they went to communion. But Wesley told them all that Christ had died for each one of them, the most wretched and the hungriest, the most ignorant and degenerate, and the wealthiest and most heartless.

John Wesley was often questioned, especially by his opponents, concerning the genuineness of the sudden conversions resulting from his preaching. Here is his answer to his questioners:

I have seen (as far as a thing of this kind can be seen) very many persons changed in a moment from the spirit of fear, horror, despair, to the spirit of love, joy, and peace; and from sinful desire, till then reigning over them, to a pure desire of doing the will of God. These are matters of fact, whereof I have been, and almost daily am, an eye or ear witness....

And that such a change was then wrought appears (not from

their shedding tears only or falling into fit, or crying out; these are
not the fruits, as you seem to suppose, whereby I judge, but) from
the whole tenor of their life, till then many ways wicked; from that
time holy, just, and good.[6]

At first Wesley confronted angry mobs everywhere he went,
mobs incited by jealous clergymen who resented Wesley's interference and by aristocrats who feared Wesley's proposal to bring
education, health, and spiritual strength to the masses of England's
poor. What would it cost the rich when Wesley convinced the poor
people of England that they, too, were human beings, children of
God?

But Wesley proved too powerful for the mobs. His preaching
convinced them that he was their friend, and they poured into
his meetings by the thousands. Wesley organized his converts into
societies for mutual encouragement in the faith. Such groups, or
"classes," the hallmark of Methodism, were organized everywhere
in the British Isles. Methodism overflowed to the American colonies
in the 1760's and proved peculiarly suited to the pioneer settlements
among which brave Methodist circuit riders traveled on their
patient horses.

But the warmth that empowered Wesley was not confined within
the Methodist movement. It reached out here, there, everywhere,
to bring life and color into the complexion of conventional Christianity. Evangelical zeal burned brightly in Protestant hearts.

A HAYSTACK AND THE ALPHABET

The evangelical zeal that warmed Wesley's heart and sent circuit
riders across the American frontier, sent men across seas to distant
Asia as well. It sent the cobbler's apprentice William Carey from
England to India as a Baptist missionary in the 1790's and David
Livingstone and Robert Moffat to Africa in the middle of the next
century.

For the beginnings of American Protestant foreign missions,
we turn to a prayer meeting in Williamstown, Massachusetts, in
the summer of 1806. Driven by an August thunderstorm to seek

shelter in the lee of a haystack, five Williams College students, among them Samuel Mills, pledged their lives to taking the gospel to Asia. The path from haystack to foreign shore was difficult, but by 1810 they had finished their schooling and persuaded their fathers and brethren in the faith to send them to India. In June, 1810, the Massachusetts General Association voted to establish the American Board of Commissioners for Foreign Missions for the purpose of sending men such as those of the haystack prayer meeting to distant shores with the good news of Christ.

On February 6, 1812, the five young men prepared to depart for India as the first missionaries of the American Board of Commissioners for Foreign Missions. The official report of the Prudential Committee of that Board, written in September of that year, describes their ordination in these words:

According to appointment, on the 6th of February, the missionaries were ordained at the Tabernacle in Salem. A season of more impressive solemnity has scarcely been witnessed in our country. The sight of five young men, of highly respectable talents and attainments, and who might reasonably have promised themselves very eligible situations in our churches, forsaking parents, and friends, and country, and every alluring earthly prospect, and devoting themselves to the privations, hardships, and perils of a mission for life, to a people sitting in darkness and in the region and shadow of death, in a far-distant and unpropitious clime, could not fail deeply to affect every heart not utterly destitute of feeling. . . . God was manifestly present; a crowded and attentive assembly testified, with many tears, the deep interest which they felt in the occasion; and not a few remember the scene with fervent gratitude, and can say, it was good to be there.

A haystack and five famous letters—ABCFM—brought American missionary zeal to fruitful focus.

A birth and baptismal certificate from Berks County, Pa., 1779

WHAT'S THE ROPE FOR?

Early on a sunny Monday morning in June, 1850, two young ministerial students—let's call them Fritz and Heinrich (hīn'rĭk)—were jogging on horseback along a Missouri road, headed for the parsonage of Pastor Joseph Rieger (rē' gĕr).

"That was a stirring appeal the pastor gave in church yesterday," remarked Fritz. "Just think, Professor Binner's family is willing to move into the new Marthasville Seminary even though the men haven't yet finished building it. They're setting up housekeeping in one of the classrooms—and nothing in the kitchen for them to eat, Pastor says."

"Well, you and I are to take care of that matter this morning," Heinrich put in. "Do you think the farmers around here will be generous with provisions?"

"They ought to be! The Evangelical people here have needed this seminary for a long time. Our families came over from Germany nearly twenty years ago, and we've had a *kirchenverein* (kērk'ĕn-fĕr'ĭn) [an organized church association] since 1840. Isn't it about time we had a school to train our ministers? The older pastors can't manage the training properly in their parsonages—not forever."

"The school would have come sooner if things hadn't been so hard for our people," Heinrich asserted. "So many had to serve terms of indenture to pay off their passages from Germany. And how many got fleeced by money changers back East? Think of the troubles our aristocratic neighbors have had trying to learn to farm this rough land. We've had little enough money to take care of ourselves, let alone build a seminary!"

"Many farmers are suspicious of the *Kirchenverein*. They remember how the state church back in Germany worked hand in glove with the government to oppress us."

Turning in at the parsonage, they saw Pastor Rieger coming out into the morning sunlight to welcome them.

"*Guten Morgen* (gōō'tĕn mōr'gĕn), boys!" he called. "The cart and the team are all ready for you to take on your rounds. I know you'll have a heavy load to pull when you wind up at the seminary this evening. Hop down, Fritz, and come over here."

The young men watched in amazement as Pastor Rieger deftly coiled a length of stout rope several times around Fritz's waist.

"What in the world is that for, Pastor? People will think I've gone daft wearing a rope around my middle!"

"Well, if they wonder about it," chuckled Rieger, "you just say that the pastor thought somebody would be wanting to give the seminary a cow."

And sure enough, when the two students got to Marthasville that night, Fritz was leading not only a cow but her calf as well.

Now, a hundred years later, the Marthasville Seminary of the old Evangelical *Kirchenverein* has grown into Eden Seminary of the United Church of Christ. It is out of the dairy business now, but still very much in the business of training new ministers.

LETTER FROM LIZZIE

In the midst of China's Boxer Rebellion, on August 3, 1900, a young American wife wrote a letter home from Fenchow:

My Dear, Dear Ones,

I have tried to gather courage to write to you once more. How am I to write all the horrible details of these days? I would rather spare you. The dear ones at Shouyang, seven in all, including our lovely girls, were taken prisoners and brought to T'aiyuan in irons, and there by the Governor's orders beheaded, together with the T'aiyuan friends, thirty-three souls. . . . We are now waiting our call home. We have tried to get away to the hills, but the plans do not work. Our things are being stolen right and left, for the people know that we are condemned. . . .

I have loved you all so much, and I know you will not forget the one who lies in China. . . . I was very restless and excited while there seemed a chance of life, but God has taken away that feeling, and now I just pray for grace to meet the terrible end bravely. The pain will soon be over. . . .

My little baby will go with me. I think God will give it to me in Heaven, . . . I cannot imagine the Saviour's welcome. . . . I do not regret coming to China, but I am sorry I have done so little. My married life, two precious years, has been so full of happiness. We will die together, my dear husband and I.

I used to dread separation. If we escape now it will be a miracle. I send my love to you all, and the dear friends who remember me.

Your loving sister,

Lizzie [11]

Twelve days later the end came for Elizabeth Graham Atwater and her husband, missionaries of the American Board. But their great vision, the vision of a world church, would live and grow.

NORWAY
King Olaf
(c. 1015)

S U

DENMARK
King Harold
(c. 950)

Columba
(c. 575)

SCOTLAND

(c. 575)

IRELAND

ENGLAND

London

Patrick
(c. 600)?

Columban (c. 600)

(c. 850)

Ansgar

Boniface (c. 720)

Rhine River

GERMAN

(c. 975)

ATLANTIC
OCEAN

Paris

Tours

Augustine
(c. 600)

SWITZERLAND
ALPS

I T A L

R

FRANCE

PYRENEES

SPAIN

MEDITERRANEAN SEA

Christianization of Europe After the Fall of Rome

0   100   200   300   400

Scale of Miles

R U S S I A

Prince Vladimir (c. 975)
· Kiev

P O L A N D
King Boleslaw (c. 1000)

E N

M I A
King Wenceslas (c. 930)

U S T R I A -
H U N G A R Y

C A R P A T H I A N
M T S.

Danube River

BLACK SEA

THE BALKANS
King Boris
(c. 865)

· Constantinople

"Love your neighbor," Jesus said. Which neighbor? Middle-class Protestants? White, native-born Americans? What do we mean by *neighbor*? Perhaps our response to Jesus' words is broader today than it would have been several generations ago, for the pleadings of Woolman and Bushnell, Gladden and Rauschenbusch have changed our thinking. *Neighbor*, they have taught us, means *all* human creatures everywhere. New studies of the Bible have underlined this revolutionary idea, and we can never again escape its impact.

JOHN WOOLMAN WINS A POINT

John Woolman was the man to talk to when trouble came—the kindly, wise, levelheaded Quaker, John Woolman of New Jersey. In the decades before the American Revolution Quakers in many of the thirteen colonies sought his leadership. He never hesitated to speak his mind in affairs great and small.

John Woolman wrote in his journal of one who sought his help:

A neighbor received a bad bruise in his body, and sent for me to bleed him, which being done he desired me to write his will. I took notes and amongst other things he told me to which of his children he gave his young Negro. . . .

I wrote his will save only that part concerning his slave, and, carrying it to his bedside read it to him, and then told him in a friendly way, that I could not write any instruments by which my fellow creatures were made slaves without bringing trouble on my own mind. I let him know that I charged nothing for what I had

done, and desired to be excused from doing the other part in the way he proposed. Then we had a serious conference on the subject, and at length he agreeing to set her free I finished his will.

The Quakers, with their firm faith that God's inner light shone in every human being, were among the first Americans to speak out against the slave trade, and John Woolman spearheaded their protest. In 1760 he urged the yearly meeting of Quakers to petition for the outlawing of the slave trade. More than a century of struggle lay ahead before slavery would be abolished, but Woolman had made his point. Christianity means respect for human rights.

St. Catherine's Monastery, Mount Sinai

THE CASE OF THE PERSISTENT PROFESSOR

The monks of St. Catherine's Monastery at the foot of Mount Sinai did not know what to make of the guest who visited them in 1844. He was an earnest young lecturer named Constantine von Tischendorf (tĭsh′ĕn-dōrf) from the University of Leipzig in Germany, and he told the monks he had come to look at their old manuscripts. They didn't understand what he wanted with their parchments, but they were willing to humor him at first. When he approached them with ill-concealed excitement carrying forty-three leaves of manuscript he had pulled out of a wastebasket, they told him he might take the trash back to Germany with him. A nuisance, thought the brother whose task it was to light the fires in the monastery. Now he would have to find something else to use for kindling.

What Tischendorf had found was a portion of the Septuagint (sĕp′tū-à-jĭnt), the Greek translation of the Old Testament, in the hand lettering of the fourth century after Christ—a manuscript as old as any yet found by 1844. Jubilantly, Tischendorf took it home to Leipzig and had it published. He came back to St. Catherine's in 1859 and spent several days begging and searching—to no avail. Sadly he abandoned his quest and packed up for the return trip. Then the story took an unexpected twist. The steward of the monas-

A portion of the fourth-century New Testament discovered by Tischendorf at St. Catherine's Monastery in 1859

tery brought Tischendorf to his cell and put into his hands a large bundle wrapped in red cloth. Inside was all the rest of the fourth-century Old Testament, and the New Testament as well. Some non-scriptural writings were also copied in the same manuscript. Here was treasure indeed! This manuscript, perhaps one of fifty ordered for the churches by Emperor Constantine himself, would show the world many secrets about how the books of the Bible had been worded by their authors; the Sinai manuscript would clear up many mistakes that had crept into the text through centuries of copying, translating, and recopying.

Tischendorf's search and his victory were part of a scientific effort in which scholars of Europe, Britain, and the United States were joining. The manuscripts Tischendorf located helped what we call textual criticism—a study of the actual text, or wording, of the Bible in an effort to discover the oldest version and the wording most nearly that of the original authors.

Many other exciting finds have been made since Tischendorf's day, the most dramatic being the discovery of the Dead Sea scrolls from 1947 on, still in their ancient jars hidden away in caves—brittle parchment covered with writing even older than the time of Jesus.

But there were also other avenues of understanding waiting to be explored. Just what did the landscape of the Bible lands look like? What was the terrain, the weather? What relics of ancient days might a wandering professor come across if he hunted? Many set out for answers, among them the energetic Dr. Edward Robinson of Union Theological Seminary in New York. He came to the Holy Land in 1838 and 1852 with his compass, telescope, thermometer, and measuring tape—and returned with a stirring new awareness of biblical geography. The settings for the vast Bible drama—from Abraham to Paul—were all quite as real as upper Manhattan!

Others searchers followed, decade after decade. Archeologists patiently picked through old ruins, discovering sometimes as many as eight cities built one on top of the other through the centuries. Sociologists studied the customs and costumes of the people of the Middle East, and realized that in that almost changeless land they would have seen much the same customs and costumes had they come when Jesus walked the roads they now traveled.

All this new study had results. Slowly the Bible took shape in people's minds as a collection of books about *real* people who had lived and pondered and suffered and died in *real* places that can still be visited. "O little town of Bethlehem, . . . we *see* thee!" People became intensely interested in Jesus as a human being. They took new interest in the words he had spoken to other human beings engaged in the perplexing business of living on this earth. The roads through Galilee became as real as roads through Massachusetts and Missouri. Nineteenth-century Christians heard with new clarity the voice of the Traveler from Nazareth.

WASHINGTON GLADDEN CHAMPIONS
THE SOCIAL GOSPEL

Two years after the close of the American Civil War a young Congregational minister named Washington Gladden was busy making plans for his installation in a church in North Adams, Massachusetts. He knew exactly whom he wanted to preach his installation sermon—Horace Bushnell, who had freed the young man's mind from what he called the "immoral theology" of a God who damned sinners to eternal hellfire.

Bushnell was afraid he would ruin Gladden's future if he

preached for the young man because many of the influential religious leaders still clung firmly to their faith in a God of wrath. But Gladden insisted, and Bushnell preached.

Gladden went on to champion Bushnell's ideas and add his own. God was a God of love, said Gladden. Man's chief business is to serve God through service to his fellowmen. No longer should Christians concentrate selfishly on saving their own souls from hellfire through emotional once-for-all conversions that did nothing to make life easier for the downtrodden underdogs of American society. No, Christians of America should look about them to see what could be done to make American business more honest, to make American communities better places in which to live.

Too many nineteenth-century churches felt quite comfortable about the money that the new machine age was pouring into their offering plates. But Washington Gladden from his pulpit in Columbus, Ohio, declared that "the church of Jesus Christ . . . is called to organize industrial and civil society on Christian principles. This is its business in the world, a business too long neglected." [14]

Encouraged by men like Gladden, church people fought for better working conditions and fairer pay in the factories and mines, for child labor laws, legal rights for women, and humane treatment of prisoners and the mentally ill. They demanded slum clearance and help for Negroes adrift in society. They championed the rights of immigrants pouring into the country. Many of these battles were not won until our own century; many are still being fought. We still need the challenge that Gladden sounded:

Because the Christian life is the noblest life; because it is more blessed to give than to receive, and better to minister than to be ministered unto; because the good of life is not found in separating yourself from your fellows, but by indentifying yourself with them—therefore, let us be Christians.

If the Church would dare to preach and practice the things which Jesus Christ commanded, she would soon regain her lost power. [14]

Gladden planted his feet firmly on Jesus' words in Matthew 25:31–46. We can do no less.

Did Washington Gladden overestimate our human ability to be decent to one another? In our generation man seems determined to blow himself off the earth, and terror stalks our world. Man's sinfulness stares us in the face. But dare we close our eyes to the glory of Christ's church in its new-strengthened oneness? Dare we ignore the great hope to which the church testifies—God's compassionate love in Christ, healing the terrible wounds we inflict on one another? Must we not join with those who hold out this hope to the world, who minister to all men everywhere in the name of the Lord of the church?

MY CHURCH: SOME TWENTIETH-CENTURY QUESTIONS

At each bend in the long road of history, we have asked: What was happening to the church here? What kind of world confronted it? What was the church saying to the world, and how was this word being spoken?

Now we ask these questions about the church of our own time. After the bright optimism of the nineteenth century with its promise of human progress toward a better world and its shining missionary hope of "the evangelization of the world in this generation," stormclouds have gathered. Two terrible world wars have reminded us that human nature is still horribly twisted by sin against God and mankind. International and interracial tensions have nearly torn the world asunder. Hate and fear, poverty, disease, and hunger grip millions of the world's people. Scientific advances threaten us with annihilation at the same time that they promise easier living in a world of plenty.

All this has reminded us that we human beings simply cannot build a better world singlehanded; we are too thoroughly enmeshed in sin for that. Only the forgiveness and power of God can enable us to do God's will on earth.

In our divided and warring world, we have realized that the bitter divisiveness within our Christian church is a sin against the Lord who called us to be one. We have sought ways to work together with fellow Christians around the globe in the mission we all share— to witness to God's love in Christ to all mankind. Where will that mission lead us? We look forward in faith for the answer.

NEW BEGINNINGS FOR PEOPLE ON THE MOVE

One summer day not long ago, a doorbell rang in the apartment of a lonely little Oriental woman in the crowded inner-city section of Cleveland. The little lady went timidly to the door, for her bell rang very seldom. Few people in Cleveland knew her; few realized that her husband was overseas in service. She lived alone with her three small children, unable to speak her neighbors' language and frightened by the unfamiliar ways of the huge city.

At her door the woman found a summer worker from Fifth United Church of Christ, part of the Inner City Protestant Parish of Cleveland, inviting her to church. Gathering up her courage, the lonely mother did come to church with her three youngsters. What's more, she began to learn English with the friendly help of a church member. The newcomer found she could share by bringing her cakes and cookies to various church activities. She could talk over her problems with her neighbors. She felt less afraid, more settled and befriended.

"God has been good to me," she remarked to her new friends. "He has given me nice children—and a new beginning."

Perhaps never before have so many people needed so desperately the new beginning that Christian fellowship has to offer. Ours is an age of people on the move, of lonely people in strange places. Each year in our U.S.A. one family in five moves to a new community. People in the downtown sections of our cities move out to the suburbs; people from rural counties grow discouraged with the prob-

107

lems of present-day farming and move to industrial jobs in the cities. Others come from depressed areas like the Appalachian south, and in an effort to find a better living, crowd into substandard, inner-city apartments in northern communities.

Too often these people who have pulled up roots find it hard to put them down again in our urban world. Jobs are scarce, especially for the unskilled; schools are crowded; and housing is inadequate and expensive. They go on and on feeling like newcomers, belonging to nobody, out in the cold. They are people without a community, almost without hope. They are part of a lonely, frightened, worldwide army of such people in our century of disrupted communities.

Many of our big downtown churches have moved to the suburbs along with their members, but churches are beginning to see their task to stay and serve the desperate needs of the new residents of inner-city neighborhoods. The work is so tough that the churches of many denominations have had to tackle it shoulder to shoulder. In Cleveland eight different denominations are working in the Inner City Protestant Parish. The Parish experiments daringly with new approaches—Sunday worship in a recreation hall or a store-front, with a noisy nursery school romping upstairs; or a weekly family fun night on a vacant lot with movies, singing, games, and worship for the people in the neighborhood. It brings help for drug addicts and juvenile delinquents, alcoholics and unwed mothers. It tries to exert pressure on recalcitrant landlords, provide tutoring for school dropouts, and initiate action against police brutality. All the ingenuity and faith of year-round pastors and summer student workers is needed to figure out what the next move should be.

How can the church today minister effectively to the people of a disturbed and lonely world? It is our mission so to minister by whatever means we can devise.

ECUMENICAL IS THE WORD

Jim and Jack were sitting on the ping-pong table, waiting for the rest of the First Church crowd to arrive for youth fellowship.

"What did they dish up at the rally last Sunday?" queried Jack.

"Sloppy joes, of course," groaned Jim. "But the food for thought was better. A fellow named Pete Blake told about being part of an ecumenical work camp in the Philippines. Said he worked all summer there with fellows and girls from all over the world, building a village community center. Said it was like living and working in a little UN, eating native food, trying to put Christianity to work. Hard work—hauling concrete blocks around—and nobody got paid; *they* paid to be there. Can you figure that? But the way Pete talked, it was wonderful. Says he has friends in eleven countries now."

"You going next summer?" Jack kidded.

Jim didn't answer, but he privately resolved to find out more about the ecumenical movement that Pete had spoken of. According to Pete ecumenicity meant all Christians praying and working as one, since all belong to the one church of Jesus Christ. This idea of the oneness of the church, Jim realized, was as old as the New Testament.

But it is modern, too—as modern as the last hundred years during which the family of denominations has been drawn closer together by the pressures of a rapidly changing world—a new world of machines, huge cities, and nightmare wars. The churches have been drawn closer together, too, by their deepening realization that the church of Christ is *one church*, not many, because it is the "body of Christ" on earth. Especially in their venture of world mission, denominations have found the need for unity. How could divided Christians make any impression on a hostile, secularized world at home or abroad? Clearly, Christians must demonstrate their essential oneness.

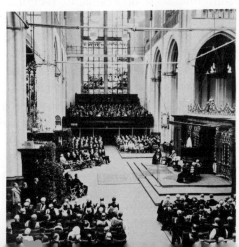

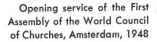
Opening service of the First Assembly of the World Council of Churches, Amsterdam, 1948

An important milestone on the road toward unity was the Edinburgh World Missionary Conference in 1910, leading to the birth of the International Missionary Council. In 1948 the World Council of Churches was born at Amsterdam to provide a framework of unity for Protestant churches around the world.

The World Council of Churches now includes not only Protestant churches, but an important non-Protestant group, the Eastern Orthodox churches which serve the people of many Balkan and Slavic countries and their descendants in the U.S. and elsewhere. People of the Orthodox faith glory in the unchanging patterns of Orthodox worship and service, feeling that Orthodoxy reflects the principles and piety of the ancient, undivided catholic church that existed before Rome and Constantinople drew apart.

In the World Council, the vigor of Protestant church life and thought and the insights of Orthodox mysticism can be translated into action through such agencies as the World Council's Division of Inter-Church Aid, Refugee and World Service. Who knows? Perhaps Jim will wield a shovel side by side with a Greek Orthodox boy when he goes to an ecumenical work camp next summer.

Ecumene is a Greek word; it means "the whole inhabited world." Certainly, *ecumenical* is a good word for our worldwide church as it seeks to bring the gospel to the whole world.

CAN WE DRAW A PERFECT CIRCLE?

Many Protestant leaders have worked hard to make our circle of Christian fellowship more nearly perfect by finding a meeting ground with the Roman Catholic Church. The Roman church has sent unofficial observers to meetings of the World Council of Churches, and in 1962 invited Protestant observers to the Roman Catholic Ecumenical Council in Rome. But there is as yet no visible unity.

Leaders of the Roman Catholic Church have always insisted that theirs is the only true church, heir of the faith of Peter and Paul and maintained through their successors, the popes. They see the Protestant Reformation as having led men away from the one true church of Christ.

110

The Roman church organized a vast missionary movement after the Reformation to win back as much of Protestant Europe as possible and to reach out daringly into the non-Christian world as well. In the great period of empire-building that followed Columbus, Portuguese and Spanish mariners brought Roman Catholic priests to Christianize the new domains in Asia, Africa, and what is now Latin America, just as the Puritans and others brought the Reformation doctrines to North America. Today the Roman Catholic Church is strong in the Philippines and everywhere "south of the border" in our own hemisphere, as well as in much of southern and central Europe.

During the nineteenth century as Latin American colonies broke away from their European masters, the Roman church lost ground there, just as it did in Europe in the rising tide of nationalism. People everywhere began to talk about separation of church and state— an idea that the Anabaptists had long championed. The idea invaded even Italy, where the Roman church lost the papal states it had controlled for centuries. The only territory now ruled by the pope is the Vatican State, a sixth of a square mile in the middle of Rome, given the church by Italy in 1929. From the Vatican the pope today guides world Catholicism.

In the United States, where the idea of the separation of church and state has long been put into practice, the Roman Catholic Church has flourished, fed by waves of newcomers from Catholic countries of Europe. Believing that Catholic children should be thoroughly educated in Catholic doctrine, the Roman church has built a system of parochial schools throughout the United States. The vigor of the Roman Catholic Church is evident from the number of its new church buildings and schools, many in arresting modern architectural style.

In recent years the Roman church has begun to put more emphasis on the importance of laymen in the church, as do Protestants. The church is training congregations to follow the mass and to join in singing the liturgy. Increasingly the Latin mass is being translated into the language of the people. Christian Action unites Catholic laymen in significant Christian witness in society.

Opening ceremonies of the second session of the Second Vatican Council in St. Peter's Basilica, Vatican City, 1963

Perhaps the Roman Catholic Church and the World Council of Churches never will or should unite, but it is significant that since the opening sessions of the Ecumenical Council in 1962, Roman Catholics are beginning to refer to Protestants not as heretics but as "brothers in Christ" and to Protestant churches as "separated churches," not as "heretical sects." Protestants and Catholics are both beginning to affirm that beneath all our differences and divisions, Christ's church everywhere in the world is now and forever one.

HOW BIG IS MY CHURCH?

At the beginning of this book we met a fictitious young man named Joe who was trying to decide how big his church was. His friendship with a young Christian from across the Pacific helped him realize that the Christian church really knows no boundaries. It is worldwide, the one great fellowship of Christians who acknowledge Christ as Lord and try to do his will.

112

The church is bigger than the boundaries of nations and denominations. It also breaks the boundaries of time. In Christ's church we have fellowship with the people of all ages who have known God's forgiving love in Christ and have made themselves instruments of God's peace, trying to do his will in the world. William W. How describes that fellowship:

> For all the saints who from their labors rest,
> Who thee by faith before the world confessed,
> Thy name, O Jesus, be forever blest.
>
> Thou wast their rock, their fortress, and their might:
> Thou, Lord, their captain in the well-fought fight;
> Thou, in the darkness drear, their one true light.
>
> O blest communion, fellowship divine!
> We feebly struggle, they in glory shine;
> Yet all are one in thee, for all are thine.
>
> And when the strife is fierce, the warfare long,
> Steals on the ear the distant triumph song,
> And hearts are brave again, and arms are strong.
> Alleluia! Alleluia!

As we read these words we are reminded of Polycarp entering the Roman arena before his death at the stake, hearing a heavenly voice crying to him, "Be strong, Polycarp, and play the man!" We think of Hugh Latimer, chained to a stake with Bishop Ridley thirteen centuries later in Bloody Mary's England, thinking no doubt of Polycarp's words as he said to his friend, "Be of good comfort, Master Ridley. Play the man. We shall this day light such a candle, by God's grace, in England, as I trust shall never be put out."

Ours is no small religion, no little church hemmed in by the limits of our own short lifetimes, for we serve Christ in the company of men like these. Our church is as wide as the world, as enduring as time itself, as strong as the love of God in Christ, not because it is ours, but because it is God's. Praise be to him!

Courtesy, Museum of Fine Arts, Boston

Almighty God, whose glory the heavens are telling, the earth his power, and the sea his might, and whose greatness all feeling and thinking creatures everywhere herald; to thee belongeth glory, honor, might, greatness, and magnificence now and for ever, to the ages of ages, through Jesus Christ our Lord. Amen.[15]

—Liturgy of St. James, second century

Almighty God, who hast given us grace at this time with one accord to make our common supplications unto thee; and dost promise that when two or three are gathered in thy name thou will grant their requests; fulfill now, O Lord, the desires and petitions of thy servants, as may be most expedient for them, granting us in this world knowledge of thy truth, and in the world to come life everlasting. Amen.

—John Chrysostom, fourth century

Too late loved I thee, O thou Beauty of ancient days, yet ever new! too late I loved thee! And behold, thou wert within, and I abroad, and there I searched for thee; deformed I, plunging amid those fair forms which thou hadst made. Thou wert with me, but I was not with thee. Things held me far from thee, which, unless they were in thee, were not at all. Thou calledst, and shoutedst, and burstest, my deafness. Thou flashedst, shonest, and scatteredst my blindness. Thou breathed odors, and I drew in breath and pant for Thee. I tasted and hunger and thirst. Thou touchedst me, and I burned for thy peace.[15]

—*Augustine, fourth century*

O eternal Light, shine into our hearts. O eternal Goodness, deliver us from evil. O eternal Power, be thou our support. Eternal Wisdom, scatter the darkness of our ignorance. Eternal Pity, have mercy upon us. Grant unto us that with all our hearts, and minds, and strength, we may evermore seek thy face; and finally bring us, in thine infinite mercy, to thy holy presence. So strengthen our weakness that, following in the footsteps of thy blessed Son, we may obtain thy mercy, and enter into thy promised joy. Amen.

—*Alcuin, eighth century*

O Lord, my God, teach thou my heart where and how it may seek for thee; where and how it may find thee. . . . O Lord, oppressed with hunger I have commenced to seek thee; let me not cease till I am filled from thy bounty, . . . poor, I have come to thy riches; miserable, to thy compassion; let me not return empty and despised. . . . Let me find thee by loving thee; let me love thee in finding thee. . . . thou hast created in me this thine image, that I may be mindful of thee, that I may contemplate and love thee; but it is so injured by contact with vice, so darkened by the vapor of sin, that it cannot attain to that for which it was created, unless thou wilt renew and reform it. . . . I seek not to understand in order that I may believe; but I believe in order that I may understand, . . . Thou art life and light and wisdom and blessedness and eternity. Amen.[15]

—Anselm, tenth century

Thy will be done on earth as it is in heaven, that we may love thee with the whole heart by always thinking of thee; with the whole soul by always desiring thee; with the whole mind by directing all our intentions to thee and seeking thy honor in all things and with all our strength, by spending all the powers and senses of body and soul in the service of thy love and not in anything else; and that we may love our neighbors even as ourselves, drawing to the best of our power all to thy love; rejoicing in the good of others as in our own and compassioning [them] in troubles and giving offenses to no one. Amen.[16]

—Francis of Assisi, thirteenth century

Refresh thy hungry supplicant, inflame my coldness with the fire of thy love, enlighten my blindness with the brightness of thy presence. . . .

Lift up my heart to thee in heaven and send me not away to wander over the earth.

Be thou alone sweet unto me, from henceforth for evermore; for thou alone art my meat and drink, my love and my joy, my sweetness and all my good.

O that with thy presence thou wouldest wholly inflame me, consume, and transform me into thyself; that I might be made one spirit with thee, . . .

Suffer me not to go away from thee hungry and dry, but deal mercifully with me, as oftentimes thou has dealt wonderfully with thy saints.

What marvel is it if I should be wholly inflamed by thee, . . . since thou art fire always burning and never decaying, love purifying the heart, and enlightening the understanding.

—from "The Imitation of Christ," fourteenth century

O Almighty and everlasting God! . . . Thou hast chosen me for this work. I know it well! Act then, O God, stand at my side, for the sake of thy well-beloved Son, Jesus Christ, who is my defense, my shield, and my strong tower.

Lord, where stayest thou! O my God, where art thou? Come! . . . I am ready to lay down my life for thy truth. . . . I will never separate myself from thee, neither now nor through eternity! And though the world may be filled with devils, though my body, which is still the work of thy hands, should be slain . . . my soul is thine! Yes, I have the assurance of thy word. My soul belongs to thee! It shall abide forever with thee. Amen. O God! Help me! Amen.

—Martin Luther, at Worms, 1521

Almighty God, our Father and Preserver! We give thee thanks that of thy goodness thou hast watched over us the past night and brought us to this day. We beseech thee strengthen and guard us by thy Spirit that we may spend it wholly in thy service. . . . Enable us, O Lord, while in labor for the body and the life that now is, ever to look beyond unto that heavenly life which thou hast promised thy children. . . . take us, O Lord, unto thy good keeping this day and all our days. Continue and increase thy grace within us, until we shall be perfectly united with the glory of thy Son, Jesus Christ, our Lord, the Sun of Righteousness . . . In whose name we pray. Amen.

—John Calvin, 1509–1564

O Heavenly Father, the Father of all wisdom, understanding, and true strength, I beseech thee . . . send thine Holy Spirit into my breast; that not only I may understand . . . how this temptation is to be borne off, and with what answer it is to be beaten back; but also, when I must join to fight in the field for the glory of thy name, . . . then I, being strengthened with the defense of thy right hand, may manfully stand in the confession of thy faith, and of thy truth, and may continue in the same unto the end of my life, through . . . our Lord Jesus Christ. Amen.

—Nicholas Ridley, 1500?–1555

What is your only comfort, in life and in death?

That I belong—body and soul, in life and in death—
not to myself but to my faithful Savior, Jesus Christ,
. . . Therefore by his Holy Spirit, he also assures me
of eternal life, and makes me wholeheartedly willing
and ready from now on to live for him.

*What do you understand by "the communion of
saints"?*

First, that believers one and all, as partakers of the
Lord Christ, and all his treasures and gifts, shall
share in one fellowship. Second, that each one ought
to know that he is obliged to use his gifts freely and
with joy for the benefit and welfare of other members.

*What is contained in a prayer which pleases God
and is heard by him?*

First, that we sincerely call upon the one true God,
who has revealed himself to us in his Word, for all
that he has commanded us to ask of him. Then, that
we thoroughly acknowledge our need and evil con-
dition so that we may humble ourselves in the presence of his majesty. Third, that we rest assured that,
in spite of our unworthiness, he will certainly hear
our prayer for the sake of Christ our Lord, as he has
promised us in his Word.[17]

—from the Heidelberg Catechism, 1562

O Christ, thou hast bidden us pray for the coming of thy Father's kingdom, in which his righteous will shall be done on earth. We have treasured thy words, but we have forgotten their meaning, and thy great hope has grown dim in thy Church. . . . Help us, O Lord, in the courage of faith to seize what has now come so near, that the glad day of God may dawn at last. As we have mastered Nature that we might gain wealth, help us now to master the social relations of mankind that we may gain justice and a world of brothers. . . .

Our Master, once more we make thy faith our prayer: "Thy kingdom come! Thy will be done on earth!" [18]

—*Walter Rauschenbusch, nineteenth century*

Listen to the heart-rending cry of Creation enslaved, corrupted, longing for peace and the reign of God.

You see what the nations have come to: their civilization and their wisdom end in a vicious circle of conflicting interests, lying and fear, armaments and wars. When will faith come to break the circle? When will God's love cover the earth?

You sense how vain are social upheavals; they are simply, as Bonaparte said, "turning over the dungheap"; the human heart remains unchanged. Who will change the heart of Man? . . .

The obstacle, the great hindrance to the spread of the gospel, is that we, its champions, have not become "sons of God." The world will believe in the power of your Master when it sees it manifested in you. Thus the whole mournful creation in a sense is waiting upon your conversion.[19]

—*Philippe Vernier, twentieth century*

HYMNS

The Church's One Foundation (Samuel J. Stone, 1866—basic to understanding the church)

Hymns from Luke's Gospel: Glory Be to God on High (*Gloria in Excelsis*), My Soul Doth Magnify the Lord (*Magnificat*), Lord, Now Lettest Thou Thy Servant Depart in Peace (*Nunc dimittis*)

O Splendor of God's Glory Bright (attributed to Ambrose of Milan, fourth century)

We Praise Thee, O God (the *Te Deum*—attributed to Ambrose and Augustine, fourth century)

Art Thou Weary, Art Thou Troubled? (eighth century Greek)

Come, Holy Ghost, Our Souls Inspire (ninth century Latin)

At the Cross Her Station Keeping (twelfth century Latin)

Jesus, Thou Joy of Loving Hearts (Bernard of Clairvaux, twelfth century)

All Creatures of Our God and King (Francis of Assisi, thirteenth century)

Jesus, Refuge of the Weary (Savonarola, fifteenth century)

A Mighty Fortress Is Our God (Martin Luther, 1529)

I Greet Thee, Who My Sure Redeemer Art (John Calvin, sixteenth century)

All People That on Earth Do Dwell (William Kethe, Scotland, 1561)

He Who Would Valiant Be (John Bunyan, seventeenth century)

Let Us with a Gladsome Mind (John Milton, 1623)

Jesus, Thy Boundless Love to Me (Paul Gerhardt, 1654)

Before Jehovah's Aweful Throne (Isaac Watts, 1719)

Soldiers of Christ, Arise (Charles Wesley, 1749)

O God, Beneath Thy Guiding Hand (Leonard Bacon, 1833)

Christ for the World! We Sing (Samuel Wolcott, 1869)

O Brother Man, Fold to Thy Heart Thy Brother (John G. Whittier, 1848)

O Master, Let Me Walk with Thee (Washington Gladden, 1879)

In Christ There Is No East or West (John Oxenham, 1908)

The Voice of God Is Calling (John Haynes Holmes, 1913)

God of Grace and God of Glory (Harry Emerson Fosdick, 1931)

Footnotes and Acknowledgments

1. From *A Source Book for Ancient Church History* by Joseph Cullen Ayer, Jr. Copyright 1913 Charles Scribner's Sons; renewal copyright 1941 Joseph Cullen Ayer, Jr.
2. From *Martyrium Polycarpi* in *Documents of the Christian Church*, edited by Henry Bettensen. Oxford University Press, New York, 1947. Used by permission of The Clarendon Press, Oxford.
3. From *The Confessions of St. Augustine*, in the translation of F. J. Sheed, Copyright 1943 Sheed & Ward, Inc., New York. Also by permission of Sheed & Ward, Ltd., London.
4. From *Benedict's Rule*, translated by Verheyen, 1906. Used by permission of St. Benedict's Abbey, Atchison, Kansas.
5. From *Translations and Reprints from the Original Sources of European History*, Vol. I, No. 2. Published by the Department of History of the University of Pennsylvania, Philadelphia, 1910. Used by permission.
6. From *Great Voices of the Reformation*, edited by Harry Emerson Fosdick. Random House, New York, 1952.
7. From *Erasmus, His Life and Character as Shown in His Correspondence and Works*. Smith, Elder, & Co., London, 1873.
8. From *The Preface to St. Paul's Epistle to the Romans* in *Luther's Works*, Vol. 35, *Word and Sacrament I*, edited by E. Theodore Bachman. Muhlenberg Press, Philadelphia, 1960. Used by permission.
9. From *Instruction in Faith* by John Calvin. Translated by Paul T. Fuhrmann. Copyright 1949, W. L. Jenkins. The Westminster Press. By permission of the Westminster Press and Lutterworth Press, London.
10. From *The Winthrop Papers, 1498–1644*, edited by S. E. Morison, Vol. I. Mass. Historical Society, Boston 1929–1944. Used by permission.
11. From *The Noble Army of Congregational Martyrs* by Albert Peel. Independent Press, Ltd., London, 1948. Used by permission.
12. From *Of Plymouth Plantation* by William Bradford, edited by Samuel E. Morison. Alfred E. Knopf, Inc., New York, 1952.
13. Paraphrased from *Through Four Centuries* by J. H. Horstman and H. H. Wernecke. Eden Publishing House, St. Louis, 1938. Used by permission.
14. From *Recollections* by Washington Gladden. Houghton Mifflin Co., Boston, 1909. Used by permission of Columbus School for Girls, Columbus, O.
15. From *The Fellowship of the Saints*, compiled by Thomas S. Kepler. Abingdon Press, Nashville, 1948.
16. From *The Writings of Saint Francis of Assisi* by Fr. Paschal Robinson. Used by permission of Dolphin Press.
17. From *The Heidelberg Catechism*, 400th Anniversary Edition, translated by Allen O. Miller and M. Eugene Osterhaven. United Church Press, 1962. Used by permission.
18. From *For God and the People, Prayers of the Social Awakening* by Walter Rauschenbusch. Pilgrim Press, Boston, 1910.
19. From *With the Master* by Philippe Vernier, published by Fellowship Publications, Nyack, N.Y. Reprinted by permission.

Credits

Grateful acknowledgment is made to the following museums, libraries, historical societies, and photographic services for permission to produce the pictures on the pages listed below.

Alinari-Art Reference Bureau, pages 9, 47
Ayosofya Museum, page 23
Bibliotheque Nationale, Paris, page 39
Bodleian Library, page 51
Courtesy of the Trustees of the British Museum, pages 13, 33, 40, 55, 72, 74
Escorial Museum, Madrid, Spain, page 35
Fogg Museum, Cambridge, Mass., page 48
Giraudon, page 56
Jerome Halberstadt, page 84
Bob Hanson, pages 3, 5, 15, 19, 88 (top right and left and bottom right)
Historical Society of York County, Pa., page 85
Franz Hogenberg, page 68
Illustrated London News, page 101
Irish Tourist Office, page 25
Lateran Museum, Rome, cover and page 22
Library of Congress, page 102
Marburg-Art Reference Bureau, pages iv, 30
Massachusetts Historical Society, page 88 (bottom left)
Municipal Archives, Rotterdam, page 77
Museum Winterthur, page 63
National Portrait Gallery, London, pages 71, 91 (top)
By kind permission of the Warden and Fellows of New College, Oxford, page 42
New York Public Library, pages 80, 86, 91 (bottom)
Philadelphia Museum of Art, pages 37, 43 (bottom), 95
Religious News Service, pages 109, 112
Dick Sanderson, pages 28–29, 98–99
Peter C. Schlaifer, page 6
Semetic Museum, Harvard University, page 34
Soprintendenza alle Belle Arte, Milan, Italy, page 21
University Library at Göttingen, page 31
Vatican Library, page 26
Eric Von Schmidt, pages 16, 17